THE ENEMY BETWEEN MY LEGS

STEPHANIE L. JONES

STEPHANIE L. JONES, LLC
The Crowned One

All Scripture quotations are from the Holy Bible, King James Version.

Cover Design: Jennifer Tyson, Indian Paper
Interior Design: Erin Howarth, Wilderness Adventure Books
Editors: Nancy McDaniel & Mary D. Edwards

This book does not necessarily represent the views of any single person interviewed in its entirety.

Published by Stephanie L. Jones
P.O. Box 401363
Redford, Michigan, 48240
www.stephanieljones.com

Library of Congress Cataloging-in-Publication Data:
Jones, Stephanie L, 1975-
The Enemy Between My Legs / Stephanie L. Jones, ~~
1st ed.   p. cm.
ISBN 978-0-9794556-0-5

2007900419
First Edition
Printed in the United States of America

To my husband: I do, we did, and will forever!

To my family: I Love You!

To every man, woman, and child: Be healed!

I also dedicate this book to my cousins,
Mario Henderson (1968-2007)
and Larry Antonio Smith (1989-2007),
and my uncle Lance Bartlett (1965-2007),
who all passed away during the final three months of
writing this book.
&
Linda "Mama Linda" Manning (1948–2003)
For loving me unconditionally!

Acknowledgments

$\mathcal{I}$ wish to thank God, my Father, who is everything to me. You are WONDERFUL! My great I AM! Yes, You are my God!

To my sweet husband, Robert A. Jones, Jr., wow! You are a solid rock in my life. Your love and support can not be expressed in words alone. I appreciate you so much. Thank you for understanding and for encouraging me to tell my story. You are a brave man! I'm looking forward spending the rest of my life loving you!

To my mother, Sharon M. Walker, I love you so much. You are a pillar of strength and a wonderful mother. I couldn't have done this without you. Donnie W. Evans, I love you heart and soul, Daddy. Thank you for always supporting me. By the way, I'm always going to be your little girl and spend your money. To my sister, April L. Henderson, no one can ruffle my feathers like you can! Thank you for always being there for me and for buying me nice clothes and for giving me expensive gifts. Keep them coming! I love you big sister! A special thanks to my father-in-law, Robert A. Jones, Sr., for always praying for me and keeping me encouraged in the Lord!

I am deeply grateful to my spiritual leadership, Bishop and Pastor Keith A. Butler, Pastor and

Minister Andre Butler, Pastor MiChelle A. Butler, Minister Kristina Butler, and the entire Word of Faith International Christian Center ministerial staff. Thank you for loving me and teaching me the Word of the God. Rev. Kenneth and Gloria Copeland, thank you for praying for me every day. I am proud to be a KCM partner. Minister Derrick Greene, thank you for ministering the "One Word from God" that literally changed my life. I want you to know that *I have staked my life on the Word of God and gone after it at all cost!*

To my friend and covenant prayer partner, Nicole B. Simpson, I couldn't imagine doing this without you. Only a true friend would get up and pray with someone every day at 6:00 o'clock in the morning. *You are my friend.* God bless you and your family.

A special thank you to Robbie Haynes, girlfriend, you lit the fire! You live and walk in righteousness. I am happy to call you friend. Angelia "Angie" White, thank you for supporting the vision. You represent what HOPE is all about.

My deepest gratitude and sincere appreciation goes to my friend, Michelle Taitt. You live in another country, with a six hour time difference, yet I can call on you *anytime* of the day or night. I love you and I appreciate your support. Jillian Blackwell—much love to you. Thank you for supporting me and letting me exhale throughout writing this book. I appreciate your prayers and friendship. Ty Adams, thank you for your prayers and encouragement. I appreciate you. Patti Toma, we were destined to be friends. Thank you for reminding me of the assignment that God has given me. Because you were obedient and shared your concerns about the first manuscript, I was able to make some last minute changes. I believe that God is pleased. Again, thank you for reminding me! I love you! To Kimberley Brooks, thank you for all of the advice and support. I admire how you "live" as a Proverbs 31 woman! Mary Edwards (Mother Mary), thank you for *everything*! You encouraged me to write this book, even when I didn't want to. I appreciate and love you! Matthew "Elder Thomas" Blacknall, I'm so happy you joined our prayer circle. Thank you for blessing me with your wisdom and love. To all of my friends who I have not mentioned by name, you know who you are, I love you!

I also wish to thank Sabrina Jackson for your support and contributing to this book. Thank you Jennifer Tyson for having patience with me and the outstanding job you did on the cover. Nancy McDaniel, you operate with a high level of integrity. Thank you for taking on this project. Erin Howarth, thank you! I enjoyed working with you. You're the best! Tavis Smiley, thank you for the advice you gave me on how to work with my family throughout this process. Last, but definitely not least, thank you Valorie Burton for writing the book *Rich Minds, Rich Rewards*. It encouraged me to tap into the power within!

Table of Contents

Like many of you reading this book, I come from a large and blended family. During my childhood, and even now in our adult interaction, we impact each others' lives in different ways. In order to protect their privacy, I've deliberately avoided providing certain details and names. Perhaps one day they will tell their story. This is mine.

Introduction

"I'm off the island," I wrote in a letter to each one of my friends. "I'm off the virgin island!" Although I was really scared about putting this type of information out publicly, I was also excited because I had just joined the elite group of popular girls. Back then, most of the popular girls in my junior high school were those who admitted they were having sex and weren't afraid to talk about it. Now I was one of them; I was 13 years old.

That experience wasn't the end of my sexual encounters as a teenager. By the time I was 22, these experiences had led to drug addiction, alcohol abuse, and low self-esteem. I now know that each time I shared my body with a man, some of whom I probably wouldn't recognize today, I was playing Russian Roulette, as if to say, "So what! Go ahead and die! He's worth the risk."

I must admit that sharing the details of the past is not easy. I have to think about things that I would much rather forget. I must reveal deep and hidden secrets that I spent most of my life protecting, especially from my parents. I must consider how my work affects my family, including those who were directly involved in the events that are revealed in this book. Yet, I can't sit idly by while people are hurting and families are being destroyed when it's within my power to help.

Many people, both children and adults, are playing Russian Roulette with their lives, but why? Why are so many people willing to risk their lives as if their lives have no value? Is it because they don't care? Of course they care. They just have so much pain bottled up inside that they'll do anything to release it. I am convinced they didn't just wake up one day and choose their lifestyles; instead, they grew into them as a result of things that happened to them over a period of time. I believe, and studies have proven, that millions of people are suffering because they have been victims of one of the most tightly-guarded secrets and covered-up crimes: child sexual abuse and molestation.

By the time you finish reading this book, child sexual abuse will have claimed the innocence of thousands of children around the world. Many will have their pride and dignity stripped away. Unless something is done to help them heal, they will quietly suffer and possibly travel down the same path of destruction that I once traveled.

In this book, I reveal the truth about a subject few people will openly talk about. It is time to do so because sexual abuse hurts everyone: male and female, rich and poor, black and white, young and old. I want the people reading this book to find hope in my story. If you or someone you know has been a victim of sexual abuse, the time has come for you to let go of the pain, shame, and guilt and begin to live a life of love, joy and freedom.

*"When men are cast down, then thou shalt say, There is a lifting up; and he shall save the humble person. **He shall deliver the island of the innocent**; and it is delivered by the pureness of thine hands."*
—Job 22:29-30

PART I
MY STORY

Chapter One

My Innocence Stolen

"The beauty of the past is that it is the past. The beauty of the now is to know it. The beauty of the future is to see where one is going."
—Unknown

How Did I Get Here?

After all of these years, it's as clear in my mind as if it happened just last week. I was about five years old, and it was a beautiful summer night. Because the weather was so nice that evening, all of us children were allowed to sleep outdoors in our sleeping bags and make-shift beds. It was a simpler time, and adult supervision wasn't necessary for such an outing. The memory of his touching me between my legs is so vivid because it was coupled with another embarrassing event; I had peed the bed. I remember lying there wrapped in those wet sheets until the next morning. I don't know if I was more ashamed of wetting myself or of the abuse that had taken place.

3

As you can see, sexual abuse didn't begin in my life like it's typically portrayed in the media, which is usually the image of an adult male hovering over an innocent little girl. My first two abusers were, in fact, quite young themselves. They were both only between 12 to 14 years old. On the outside they appeared to be normal young men. They attended school, played sports, chased girls, and hung out with their friends. They were very nice to me, too. I was around them often, and I thought of them as my big brothers. In fact, I loved them.

Since I was only five years old when the sexual abuse with these young men began, I can't say that I remember all of the intimate details about it, such as whether there was intercourse or oral sex. Having spent so much time lately digging into my past, I find it interesting how much the mind will suppress in order to avoid pain. However, I know without a doubt that I was molested by these young men, especially the older one. I remember spending a lot of time with him in his bedroom kissing him, fondling, rubbing, and grinding on his legs and penis. Usually, I was on top of him following directions as a kid is taught to do. I remember very little about the abuse with the second young man, except for the bed-wetting experience mentioned above and that it was ongoing over a period of time.

I was between 7 and 12 years old when the molestation began with other people, and for a long time, I assumed that this was the beginning of the abuse. I had no idea that it went back as far as age five. I had buried the events with the two young men deep in my subconscious. At some point I even questioned whether or not it happened, but I know it did. The memories of it have always haunted me. There was a two-year period in my life that I had recurring images of a man on top of me. I knew that it was someone different, not one of my offenders whom I already knew about. Here is a letter that I wrote several years ago about these images.

> *I have images in my head. There are images of me lying in bed next to a man. There are also images of me on top of him. The images are real and powerful, but this man's touch is unfamiliar. It's not like the others. It's not one that I'm used to. So many times over the years I've tried to see his face, but I can't. Was there sexual penetration? How about oral sex? I don't know. I just don't know.*

I knew that it was someone I least expected. His presence was very strong. It was as if I could literally still feel his touch, but I couldn't see his face. I tried to guess who it was, but I kept drawing a blank. Then one day out of nowhere, a very familiar face, one that I hadn't seen in years, appeared in my mind. It was like someone was holding a photograph or a police mugshot in front of my eyes and saying, "This is him." I knew immediately who it was. I knew that it was the young man who was the first person to sexually abuse me, the one I looked up to like a brother. Being able to finally see his face answered so many questions for me about the past and how the abuse began in the first place.

I can't really say why I didn't tell back then. Obviously these were people I cared about, and I didn't want to get them in trouble. Maybe that's what kept me quiet for so long. It could've been that my own curiosity just got the best of me, and I didn't want to tell. Perhaps it felt good to me, and I didn't want it to stop. It could've been one or a combination of reasons. Although I didn't know the seriousness of the situation at the time, I knew that it was wrong, not because someone had told me that it was; I just knew. Even as a young child I knew how to act, what not to say and do, and how to pretend that all things were normal between me and these young men. I knew to jump up and pull up my little pants or pull down my little dress when a door would suddenly open or when footsteps were approaching. I knew never to tell anyone, and until now, I never did. I never told a soul.

To think that I had my first sexual experience at only five years old is unimaginable. I often wonder what I knew at five. Could I recite my ABCs without singing them? How far was I able to count? What was my favorite doll's name? Did I know how to ride my bike without training wheels? Undoubtedly, my concerns were much greater than these. I had more serious matters to contend with.

Even after having experienced sexual abuse for many years, writing about it and speaking about it around the world, it's still hard for me to fathom the idea of a five-year-old child engaged in a sexual act with a teenager or an adult man or woman.

The House That Sharon Built

One of the many questions I'm often asked is where my parents were when the sexual abuse was going on, so I want to address this subject early on. I must be honest and admit that if the tables were turned and I was reading this story instead of sharing it, it would probably be the number one question on my mind, too. "Where in the world were this girl's mother and father, and did they know about it?"

I have great parents. They are wonderful people who love me, and I love them. They are two of my best friends. The bond that I share with them is very special and has been throughout my life. As a matter of fact, the bond keeps getting stronger over the years. My parents have always encouraged me to reach for my dreams and accomplish my goals.

However, I would be less than truthful if I told you that things were always good in our household. Obviously, there was some negligence on their part. My father did the father stuff, such as teaching me how to cook and coming to school events, but he definitely didn't do the daddy stuff. He didn't get involved with my personal development. I don't recall our having conversations about the clothes I wore, the friends I hung out with, where I was spending my free time, or the young men that were calling or stopping by to visit me. We never had a single conversation about sex. These are very critical areas in which a daughter needs her father to be involved, and my father wasn't.

Coming from a broken home herself, my mother did

the best she could at that time. She was very much on her own and taking care of herself and her siblings from the time she was 14 years old. She never had the opportunity to learn parenting skills before becoming a parent herself, but she definitely was more involved in my personal life than my father was. My mother had a lot of faith in me. I think she just accepted what I told her because I was the "good girl." I didn't fit society's profile of a troubled teen. I was a straight "A" student whom everyone considered perfect. I rarely got into trouble, and that kept my mother content. But as the saying goes: Never judge a book by its cover!

Though I can explain, I can't paint a true picture of what growing up in our house was really like. Having been homeless herself, my mother didn't like to see people without a place to live. Therefore, we sometimes had 10 to 15 different people living with us at one time. *The House that Sharon Built*, as we affectionately called it, included relatives, friends, neighbors and homeless people. Our home had a revolving door; people came, people went, and then came back again. Although her intentions were good and her heart was right, these living arrangements left me exposed to all kinds of things that a child should never see, hear, or be around, including drugs, alcohol, gambling, and sex. These things became the norm to me; they were a part of my life and played a major role in the choices that I would eventually make.

I used to be really angry with my parents for bringing me up in such a horrid environment. But, now that I'm old enough to understand, I realize that most of what was going on around me simply trickled down from generational problems that have existed in my family for years. I recently learned that both my grandmother and great-grandmother suffered many years of severe physical abuse from my great-grandfather. Eventually, this led to my grandmother living on the streets at a very young age. By the age of 32, she had 12 children and had become an alcoholic. She died when she was just 40 years old, leaving her children without a stable place to call home. This is one of the reasons why we always had so many people living with us.

I don't know much about my father's parents' marriage, except that it ended in a bitter divorce when he was a young man. I've heard some frightening stories about what happened, but my father doesn't talk about it, so I no longer ask.

I'm sure you're wondering if my parents knew about the abuse. The answer is no. I know for sure that neither one of them knew about it. That may seem impossible, but like so many other parents, they didn't recognize the signs of child sexual abuse or simply dismissed them as something benign. Besides, they never expected something like this to happen to their child. They would have never imagined that the very people they call brother and friend could do such horrible things to their little girl. Despite the fact that the abuse usually happened in our home and sometimes when they were just a few feet away—in the kitchen cooking a meal, in their bedroom, or outside talking with a neighbor—I know they had no idea what was happening to me. Most of it is being revealed to them within the pages of this book.

What Did My Parents Have To Say About All Of This?

Not long after my 29th birthday, I dropped what seemed like a deadly bomb on my mother. With a few carefully selected words, my nightmare became her reality. I had already settled in my spirit that I was going to tell her about the abuse, but I didn't expect it to be so difficult. Thankfully, the night before I'd heard Bible teacher and best-selling author Joyce Meyer talk about the importance of getting the hard stuff over with in order to move on in life. She described it as rocking back and forth like preparing to jump between two ropes for a round of Double Dutch. "At some point, you just have to jump in there," she said. That night I sat on my mother's couch rocking back and forth for hours.

Since my mother and I have always spent a lot of time together, she didn't find it strange that I was taking up so much of her time with idle conversation. More than three hours went by before the words flew out of my mouth, and when they did, it was as if the ton of bricks that had been resting on my chest for years was finally lifted. My mother broke down crying. She said that she had let me down and hadn't protected me. That still hurts me today because I know that she loves me very much. I knew that she would be totally devastated, so I was prepared to combat her anger with some scriptures on healing and forgiveness. Most importantly, I could honestly look her in the eyes and say, "Mom, it's okay. Look at the woman I am today. It is well."

There's not much to say about my father and his finding out. As I expected, things went much easier with him. He asked two questions: "What are you talking about?" and "Why didn't I know about this before now?" Still today, he doesn't talk about it. He was caught totally off guard with all of this, and I believe he's still in a state of shock and denial. To him, I'm still his little girl, so I could only imagine how difficult this must be for him to handle. I think not talking about it is his way of dealing with his own pain and feelings of guilt.

As of today, neither one of my parents has confronted any of the people who were abusing me. Since my parents are no longer in a relationship together, my father's relationship with certain family members and the people that I was close to as a child is drastically different. He rarely sees them and chances are, some of them he will never see again. My mother is not ready to confront anyone. This has been really hard for her to deal with. I haven't even told her who all of my perpetrators were. I will tell her when she's ready.

Although neither of my parents knew about the sexual abuse, a lack of responsibility played a major role in what happened to me as a child. However, I've forgiven them both and moved on. Being able to forgive my parents and strengthen my relationship with them has been one of the greatest benefits of opening up about the abuse. Many abuse victims never come forward. They quietly seethe in anger and blame their parents for it. However, I refused to become a victim twice.

Chapter Two

The Aftermath

Stephanie, Thou Art Loosed!

The 2004 release of the movie *Woman Thou Art Loosed* stirred my soul and brought memories flooding back. I sat in the movie theater next to my husband feeling very uncomfortable. I had a lump in my throat, and tears were constantly welling up in my eyes. The movie was about a young girl who was molested by her mother's boyfriend. As an adult, the sexually-abused victim, played by the great actress Kimberley Elise, eventually killed her abuser. It haunted her thoughts throughout her entire life, and she just couldn't seem to let it go. Yes, it was only a movie, but similar scenes play out in homes across the world every single day. I personally endured over seven years of sexual abuse by many different people. Can you imagine what it's like to be sexually abused by so many people that you forget who they all are and who did what?

After the movie ended, I remember thinking there

would be so many people who would view the movie and not understand it. For some people it would be just another entertainment flick. Some would think that by killing her abuser she went a bit overboard, especially for something that happened to her as a child. Yet, I understood her pain and her reaction. This is not to say that I agreed with it. Taking a person's life is not the answer, but I understood how she got to that point of rage. Wounds that go unhealed, along with all of the other pressures of life, can make the strongest person lose control. As my husband is always telling me, "Pressure busts pipes!"

Junior High School: Nothing But Pressure

I was always book smart, and I hungered for knowledge. From the start of elementary school, I was a straight "A" student, and I remained one throughout most of my school years. However, this put a lot of pressure on me. My parents, their friends, and other family members showered me with gifts and money. Every day people were asking me or telling me what I was going to be when I grew up. Talk about pressure! In fact, there was so much pressure on me that early in life I learned to walk, or at least pretend to walk, a straight line. I felt like I had to always have it together. I dared not let anyone see that things were not well with me, that I was terribly afraid to bring home even a "B" on my report card, and that I suffered from low self-esteem. I couldn't let anyone know that my own relatives and friends of the family were feeling on my body and violating me in the worst type of way. What would people think about me? They would know that I wasn't perfect after all.

By the time I made it to junior high school, the role playing became second nature to me. I was the 7th grader who always felt extremely out of place. I didn't like the way I looked or the shape and size of my body. I thought that I was fat and ugly, and I would do almost anything to make new friends. In order to mask the pain, I kept myself busy and mingled among the who's-who crowd. Although I felt insecure in their presence, I always made sure that I hung out with the popular girls. I wanted their hair, their looks, and their life-styles. They didn't seem to have chaos in their homes and in their lives like I did, so I hung out with them because that meant that I would be considered cool and popular, too.

I was still being molested during those years. As a matter of fact, it went on more during that time than any other. It is that time period that I remember the most. I was molested by several different people while I was in junior high school. The sexual abuse became so prevalent in my life that by the time I turned 13 and entered the 8th grade, I wanted to have sex because I had become accustomed to it and the way it made me feel physically. It was something that I was familiar with, and I began to see it as a means to an end. It was a way to get the attention that I was used to and des-perately wanted. Sex quickly became like a cash com-modity to me, a source of payment to get the material things that I desired. I found out at a very early age that sex had a certain amount of power to it, and I was willing to use it.

Mindless and fearless of the consequences and danger of what I was doing, I also started drinking while I was in junior high school. Some of the older people that I hung out with would buy liquor for me and my friends. So, on a regular basis, I was supplying and drinking alcohol at after school parties. When I was in the 7th and 8th grades, people were still having basement and backyard parties, so it was easy for us to sneak the liquor into people's houses without their parents noticing.

While this craziness was going on, I walked perfectly in the sight of others, especially my parents. I wrote for the school newspaper, successfully competed in academic competitions, and continued to bring home good grades. Other than a couple of incidents, like starting a food fight in the school's cafeteria, I didn't give my parents any problems.

Well, there is one other incident that should have been a huge sign that something wasn't right. When I was in the 7th grade, my friends and I were planning to have a party. Everyone in the school was talking about it. At 7:00 A.M., on the morning of the party, we met on the corner where the school bus picked us up and drunk several bottles of cheap liquor. By the time the bus arrived, we were stone cold drunk. The school's administration quickly found out because the smell of alcohol was seeping from our pores. We stunk! They also knew something was wrong because my friends were vomiting and couldn't stand up straight. I didn't get caught, but someone ratted me out because I was the one who brought the alcohol to the bus stop. Although I was suspended from school, my parents didn't even punish me. They considered this type of behavior completely out of character for me and within days, it was as if it never happened.

Grown Man, She's Too Young For You; Little Girl, He's Too Old For You!

I was also dealing with another serious issue in junior high school, my attraction to men who were much older than I was. Because most of the sexual abuse came at the hands of older teens and adults when I was a young girl, I was drawn to them once I got older. Of course, I was more attracted to adult men than teenage boys. I had a crush on a few boys that I went to school with, but none of them ever seemed to like me. I blamed it on my weight and my looks. My butt wasn't big enough, my breasts were too small, and my hair didn't flow down my back like the pretty girls. If boys didn't show the slightest bit of interest in me, I felt rejected, and it would send me into deep states of depression and back into the arms of men who always seemed to be attracted to me.

Although I did have a couple of relationships with boys my age, it was really just to pass the time. At 14, my so-called boyfriend was 18 and a high-school senior. At 16, I began seeing a man 23, and at 17, there was a man who was 30. At 19, I became involved with a man 34 and then one 38. Being with older men somehow made me feel important and presented the challenges I thought I needed. Older men always knew what to say to make me feel good and grown. They used to say things to me like, "Oh, you're just a baby." "I don't want to use a condom because I need to feel you." And let's not forget those three powerful words we all long to hear, "I love you." It all sounded good to me.

There was one thing that always bothered me in those relationships. Of course it sounds silly to me now, but I was irritated that none of the men would commit to a serious relationship with me. What I really wanted was a boyfriend like all of the other girls had, but these men didn't take me out to the movies or hold my hand when we were together. They didn't hang out with me and my friends or buy me cards and teddy bears on Valentine's Day. They never took me around their families or friends. I was never invited to a holiday dinner or family celebration. We were never seen in public together. It was all about the sex. I don't know what we even talked about back then. What could our conversations have been about other than what they wanted to do with me and to me sexually?

Today, I often find myself trying to explain to young girls the need to closely evaluate and get out of their relationships with older men. I'm dealing with young girls who are 15 and 16, and they're involved with men 21 to 25 years old and some older. Everything about them should be different, from the programs they watch on television to the music they listen to and the type of books they read. Most young girls though are always hard to convince. Being with older men seems to give girls some brownie points with their friends and make them think they are grown. In reality, they're just little girls involved in grown folks' business, and the men are just males who are considered men because of their age. They are males robbing young girls of their child-hood. They're committing statutory rape, but that's another subject altogether. Many of them use young girls to boost their egos because they can't handle a serious relationship with a woman their own age. I wish that someone had come along and asked me, "Stephanie, you're 16, and he's 23. If he's with you, what should that tell you about him?"

High Heels and High School

I didn't have the traditional high-school experience. Despite what some people might think, I didn't even enjoy those years. I was dealing with too many issues in my personal life that weighed me down emotionally. Not long ago, I ran into an old classmate who said to me, "No one understood you back then. You were always so grown and ahead of the rest of us. A lot of people didn't like you because of that, especially the girls."

Most of my time spent in high school is a complete blur to me. I was there but not really there, if that makes any sense at all. If there was any other time period of my life that I could do over again, it would be my high-school years. I would take the time to do more of the things girls do in high school and allow myself to be a kid. In high school I was into grown folks' business and doing things that I didn't have any business doing. But I did try really hard to fit in. I went to school pep rallies and basketball games, and I even tried to mesh with cliques, but I found it hard to bond with them. I thought the girls in high school were into kid stuff, and I probably treated them like it, so we clashed often. To be honest, although I envied what they had, I actually looked down on the other kids in high school. I used to think they were silly and immature. I thought my fancy hair, extra long fake fingernails, and high-heel shoes made me a woman. What I really enjoyed doing was going home and standing out on the corner with the older people in the neighborhood.

Even so, I was still a good student. I think that's important to reiterate. So often people think that a person must show disruptive behavior to be in trouble, but that wasn't me at all. I kept my grades up, and I was active in student associations. I liked participating in the student groups, too. I was a member of the Literary Arts Club, National Honor Society, Students Against Drunk Driving (SADD), and I served on the yearbook committee and was voted a senior class officer. However, on the flip side of all of this, I had grown men picking me up from school, and I sneaked and got my first tattoo when I was in the 11th grade. When things came up like the homecoming dances, I never had a date, so I always went with one of my male friends whom I just hung out with, or I went with a group of girls who didn't have dates either. Of course the men I was talking to wouldn't dare be seen at a 10th or 11th grade high-school dance.

Looking back, high school was the loneliest and most confusing time of my life. It's when the depression really kicked in. I didn't feel loved, and I wanted to be held and to feel some type of affection. I attempted to cover up my feelings with material possessions and with trying to look good. I was spending almost $100 a week, money I earned at my after school job and what my parents gave me, on looking cute, and this was back in high school. I got a lot of attention, and that's when I began feeling like these things made me a better person and made people like me more. In high school, there is such overwhelming pressure to fit in, to wear the latest styles, and to have all of the popular gadgets. I was feeling pressure on every side: at home, at school, externally and internally.

Of course, the material things couldn't give me the love that I missed and so desperately wanted to feel. By my senior year, I had separated myself from everyone but a few people who tolerated my moody behavior and who thought that I acted like an old lady anyway. Soon, I began having suicidal thoughts. I was frustrated with my looks, my body, and my relationships. Nothing seemed to be going right in my life.

Graduating: On To the Next Level

In the fall of 1994, I enrolled in Eastern Michigan University. I was the first person in my family to attend a college or university. People were excited and expected me to make them proud. Boy, did I disappoint them. The many years of abuse and feelings of depression and loneliness followed me everywhere I went. College life was horrible. In no way was I prepared to be on my own, not mentally and definitely not emotionally. I just let go and let loose. Actually, being away eased the pressure quite a bit. I no longer had to tiptoe around my family pretending that I was someone I wasn't. It made it easier for me to be a real naughty girl because they were not around, and they couldn't see what I was doing. At last, there was no one to hide from. Away at school, I was doing everything but focusing on my education. Within three months, I found myself on probation for my rowdy behavior; by the end of the first semester, I was also on academic probation.

I quickly gained a reputation on campus for being the party girl, the one who was always drunk, high, or both. I was known for wearing nice clothes and spending lots of money. I indulged in alcohol, marijuana, and expensive clothes and jewelry. I would attend "get-high parties" with my friends, where everyone was responsible for bringing bags of marijuana and bottles of liquor and beer. If people couldn't get a hold of these things themselves, then they just chipped in their five or ten dollars. For hours, we would play cards, smoke, and drink. Sometimes we weren't allowed to leave the room unless we finished all of what we brought with us, and that was on top of smoking and drinking some of what everyone else had brought.

There were days that I didn't know whether I was coming or going. One night I passed out on the floor of a dorm mate's bathroom. Everyone was so high that still to this day no one knows how long I was in there. Like that night and so many others, I had pushed the envelope as far as I could, and my body just gave up. Many people have died from these types of drinking parties. My life was spared every time. This is just one of the many nights that God wrapped me in His arms and kept me alive, even before I knew Him.

Life was wild at Eastern Michigan. I was popular back in high school, but it was not the same. Everyone knew me on campus, and I just loved it. The attention felt good, and because I didn't have the least bit of sense, I enjoyed feeling like all eyes were on me. I thought it made me someone special. There's something addictive and sickening about the need for attention. It makes people do stupid things. I guess that I was acting in my own personal reality show back then, long before they even became popular on television. I felt that as long as people noticed me on the outside, they would never have a clue about the broken-down girl living on the inside.

I worked hard to keep up this charade. I needed a spotlight beaming down on me at all times in order to feel that I was somebody. I was spending all of my savings and the money that my parents faithfully gave me every week getting high and trying to keep up with the Joneses. During the day, while most of my hanging buddies were in class, I would get high and go shopping at the mall. It was another way for me to keep busy since I wasn't going to class myself. I recall one of my friends asking me, "You have just one class, right? What, you can't make it to that one class?" At the time I thought it was funny and just laughed at him. The only reason I was still enrolled in that one class in the first place was so that I wouldn't get kicked out of the school and off campus.

With the amount of money I was spending partying and trying to look good, I found myself swimming in credit card debt by the end of my freshman year. I accepted every card I was offered by the credit card companies conveniently stationed all around the campus, and I was spending much more money than I was bringing in. Needless to say, I didn't survive long at Eastern Michigan. I dropped out after just one year. In the past, I tried to convince myself that things only ended up so bad there because I didn't get the chance to attend Howard University, which is where I really wanted to go. In reality, though, I know that the situation would have ended up the same wherever I crash landed.

On top of all the baggage that I took with me, I wasn't prepared for college life. In my condition, entering an environment free of parental control and being surrounded by young adults experiencing this same freedom was like living in hell. I just couldn't handle the temptations that were all around me.

Chapter Three

Transitioning–
Somebody Dial 9-I-I!

Back Home Again

J don't remember what reason I gave my parents for coming back home. Whatever it was, they trusted me and didn't question my decision. After all, I was their straight "A" student and their perfect little girl. I had managed to graduate from high school with honors, keep a job, and go to college. I guess they figured that I knew what I was doing.

Once I got settled back in at home, I really tried to slow down and do the right thing. Because I withdrew from all of my classes and got an "E" in the one class I was enrolled in, I couldn't gain acceptance into another university, so I enrolled in the local community college. I started attending school full-time again and working a full-time job. I remember feeling pretty good about myself. I thought that somehow I'd managed to walk away from everything that had happened during the previous 14 years, especially during the last 10 months at Eastern Michigan. At that time all appeared to be well. But there's a big difference between things being well and appearing to be well. I still had one very big problem. I wasn't well on the inside. Although I wanted to do right, I didn't really know what right was. Not to mention, people doing the wrong stuff seemed to be having all of the fun. I also wanted to have fun and just couldn't seem to resist getting into trouble. So one very hot summer day, I went boldly knocking on trouble's door.

Knock-Knock: Who's There? Trouble!

Although I was working really hard at my new job and working diligently to keep my grades up, it didn't take long for me to hit the streets again. Partying and getting high had become a part of my nature.

One day, while out having *fun*, I met a guy and immediately found myself trapped in a relationship that almost cost my life.

At face value, this guy appeared to be everything that I wanted. He was rough and tough and wore his pants sagging down below his butt. He had a lot of diamonds hanging around his neck and on his fingers. His car was sitting on $5,000 rims, and his music could be heard a block away. He was as high as a kite the day we met. He was perfect for me. It didn't take long before I became his girl and soon found myself on his arm at all times. There wasn't much for us to talk about. He didn't have a job, and besides getting high we didn't have a whole lot in common. I don't know how, but I actually stayed in that relationship for over two years. I was totally infatuated with him, and he became the most important person in my life. My family, my friends, school, and my career took a backseat.

The relationship was a rough one. We were constantly fighting. He was cheating on me; of course I stayed. He *thought* I was cheating on him; of course he left. I would all but get on my knees and beg him to come back. The relationship was on a road to nowhere. It started out that way and it stayed that way.

At some point, he became violent. In the beginning he would only threaten me. On several occasions, he told me that he could easily end my life. I believed him. Ever since I'd known him, he'd slept with a loaded Glock handgun under his pillow. It wasn't long before he started pushing me and grabbing my face while backing me into a wall. Eventually, he started slapping me and knocking me upside my head. I really wanted out at that point. I had always said I would never let a man beat on me, yet I endured the painful abuse until he almost killed me. I wanted out, but I was too afraid to leave him.

One night in a drunken rage, he tried to kill me. He hit me one time. The blow sent me flying across the room like a rag doll. He then jumped on top of me, put his knee in my chest, and choked me until I passed out. I could hear him calling me all kinds of obscene names and telling me to die as my life slowly slipped away.

My life was spared again that night, but by the time it was over, I had been knocked unconscious, my mother's life was threatened, and two doors and a 50-gallon aquarium were left shattered. Both I and my tropical fish lay sprawled out on the floor gasping for air. He didn't leave our house easily that night, but all that matters is that he left. Thank God he left.

On The Rebound

That was a close call, but it still wasn't enough for me to change my ways. The following few years only got worse. Although I did somehow manage to graduate with a 3.8 GPA, earn my associate's degree, and get a new job at the phone company making a lot more money, I simply replaced my ex with different men whom I met at parties and clubs. I was hanging out with a whole new group of young ladies, all of whom wanted to party as much as I did. So that's exactly what we did. We partied seven days a week; there were the Monday-Night-Football parties, $2-dollar Tuesdays, All Jokes Aside Comedy Night on Wednesdays, Ladies Night on Thursdays, a cabaret on Fridays, and a number of clubs to choose from on Saturday and Sunday nights. We never missed a party!

For the next three years I partied hard. If there was something going on, I had to be there. Sometimes we would stand outside during a freezing Detroit winter, 10 degrees below zero, 3-inch sandals, lace shirts and mini skirts that would show it all if we sneezed, no panties, no bras and no coats, waiting in line for hours just to get into the club. Oftentimes I wore the most provocative thing I could find just to get men's attention and have them look at me.

By this time I was smoking so much marijuana and drinking so much alcohol that I could no longer function without it. I kept bottles of liquor stashed in my room and in the glove compartment and trunk of my car. Words alone can't explain what I was doing to myself.

The only time that I wasn't high, drunk, or both was when I was at work, but even then I was drinking in my car or at a restaurant on my lunch breaks.

Day after day and night after night, the routine never changed. I still had the same bad habits. I was willing to accept anything and anyone just so that I could have some type of man in my life. It was during this time that I sunk to an all-time low in how I let men treat me and how I treated myself, but I didn't care. I had a new crew of girlfriends, a new car, a whole lot of new clothes, and a new job. Of course, more money earned meant more money to spend for me and my friends. I paid our way into clubs, made sure we always had stashes of marijuana, and took care of the bar tabs if necessary. I felt like the queen bee. I thought this made my friends love me and look up to me, and I was desperate for love and attention.

I went to the mall to shop almost every single day because I felt that I could never wear the same thing twice. The mall employees knew me by name and that I was always coming to spend big. I was known for looking good, and I couldn't let the people down.

My life was a disaster. I put on the biggest charade for my family and co-workers. I refused to let anyone know what was really going on. The alcohol and drugs gave me the ability to easily slip in and out of character. They gave me the courage to do things that I was too ashamed to do without them. I can't put a dollar amount on how much this habit was costing me. It varied daily depending on how bad I was feeling, where I was, whom I was with, and what we were doing. Some days I was drinking more than a fifth of liquor straight from the bottle, no chaser.

To this day, I thank God that my liver is still functioning. I'm thankful that I made it home safely every time I got behind the wheel while I was drunk. I could have been responsible for killing your mother, your father, or perhaps your entire family. I'm thankful for the young man who woke me up at four in the morning as I sat passed out drunk behind the wheel in the middle of a major road. The Bible says that we entertain angels unaware (Hebrews 13:2). He was definitely my angel that morning. I thank God for the security guard who recognized my car and watched over it for an entire night. I was so drunk that I had jumped out of my car at two in the morning and left it parked, running on keyless ignition until eight in the morning.

I thank God that my life was spared each time I bought drugs from a complete stranger with no idea of what type of additional substances had been added to them. Although marijuana was beginning to lose its effect on me, every now and then I would get a hold of something laced with another substance that would have me out of my mind. Those substances never killed me or did any physical damage. Some people have a different story to tell, if they're alive to tell it at all.

Sick and Tired of Being Sick and Tired

Have you ever awakened and felt tired and depressed about the direction your life was taking? You really want things to change, but you don't know where to begin, and you're afraid of what change might look like. On the other hand you feel like the world has never showed you any love, so maybe you should just keep doing what you're doing. After all, you know about the life you're currently living. You're accustomed to the people, the places, the ups and the downs. It's all a part of you.

That was me. I definitely knew all about the life I was living. I had become familiar with living life in the fast lane and on the wild side. But no matter how accustomed I had become to living in it, I was really tired of it and didn't want to live it anymore. I was sick and tired of being sick and tired. I was tired of feeling as if I needed a man to make me feel like I was important. The party scene became boring to me, and the drugs and alcohol were not helping me at all. In fact, they were making things worse. In reality, I was involved in another abusive relationship, just not with a man. This time I was abusing myself. Again, I wanted out.

I started passing up on the parties and staying home most nights. It took a while, and it was a struggle for me, but eventually I stopped getting high also. It wasn't a quick transition for me, but my life calmed down. I took it one day at a time. It was like having one foot in the box and one foot out. I often describe it as taking an animal out of the wild and suddenly caging it in a zoo. I had to adapt to the new life that I was trying to live.

The more effort I put into changing my life, the easier it became. I was spending a lot of time alone because I felt I needed to be by myself. I had gone through a lot of *friends* and *boyfriends*, and experienced many episodes of a broken heart, so I stopped dating altogether. It hurt my feelings and took me some time to get over it, but of course my friends and I easily went our separate ways. I was no longer fun to hang around, and I was no longer the queen bee. I entered into a period of rest, and it was during this time that I found some peace. It was also during this resting period that my life would change forever. I became spiritually connected with a long-time friend who would eventually become my best friend and my husband.

Bad Boys

I've been asked many times, "Stephanie, did you like Robert when you were growing up?" People always find it surprising that my answer is no, considering that we'd practically been next-door neighbors since we were five and eight years old. I didn't like my husband back then, not in a personal way. He was all right to talk to, but that was about it. He was too quiet and didn't cause trouble in our neighborhood. He had a real job. I can still picture him walking down the block in his work uniform. No, I didn't like him at all. He was all wrong for me, too nice, too respectful; he wasn't a rough and tough troublemaker.

I didn't want anything to do with a nice, working young man. I wanted a bad boy in my life, the type of man I was being entertained by and hearing about in the music that I listened to and watched in the videos that were on T.V. He had to drive a certain type of car, dress a certain kind of way, and portray a certain type of image. I liked being involved with the petty drug dealers that I knew. Back then I associated drug dealers and troublemakers with strength and protection. I thought these were the types of guys that would protect me from any danger that came my way. The truth is, they put me in more dangerous situations than I care to admit. I must also say that I got involved with these types of men because I wanted to impress my friends. When I was growing up, girls seemed to envy and look up to other girls who were involved with the bad boys. Just like much of everything else that I did, who I was going out with was all about keeping up my image.

I Do: The Two Famous Words We All Long To Hear

I know that God saved my husband just for me, but if you ask my mother she'll tell you that it was all her doing. "I picked my own son," she proudly says. In a way, there's some truth to that. After all, we'd known each other almost our entire lives and until we started dating, we really were just friends. It was only after my mother invited Robert, her favorite young man in the neighborhood, to travel along with us on our annual family vacation that things became serious between us. I remember looking at her like she'd lost her mind when she asked him to join us. I felt relieved when he looked as shocked as I did and brushed her off with a shy smile. Yet my relief soon turned back into shock when I saw him walking down our block with a duffle bag tossed over his shoulder as I was loading my luggage into the car the following week.

As teenagers and young adults we had spent countless hours sitting on my porch talking about our dreams, the hotels we would someday own, and how rich we were going to be when we got older. But it never went any further than friendly conversation. However, during that family vacation, we connected on a new level. It was the first time I saw him as more than just Robert from down the street.

My life did a 360 degree turn when Robert and I started dating; everything changed. It wasn't easy, but eventually I stopped drinking, which was a bit harder than giving up the drugs. With alcohol being legal, it was easier to come by. It was just a matter of my pulling over at the nearest corner store or wherever alcohol is sold. Kicking the addiction all together was a serious struggle for me, and it didn't happen overnight. At one point I convinced myself that I could drink wine every day because doctors said that it was good for me. I also told myself that there was nothing wrong with my doing so because I had heard that Jesus turned water into wine, so it must be okay. Without understanding this particular Bible story, I used it to help me along and bandage up my problem until I learned better.

All while Robert and I were dating, he knew that I was working out some personal issues, but he never pressured me into revealing what was going on. He just toughed it out with me. We started going to church together, which was a big change from what I was used to. I had been to church many times before, but never with a man. It was the first time that I really enjoyed going to church, and I was going for the right reasons: to see what God and not someone else had to say about who I was. Eventually, it became the only place that I wanted to be, and I was going with and without him. Not only was I attending services on Sundays, but I was also going on Wednesday nights. What a change! I felt really at peace when I was there. I soon found out that there is a God that loves me more than anyone in this world ever could, and despite everything that had happened in the past, I was still capable of living a normal, happy, and peaceful life. I felt like life was finally doing me right and that I was going to be okay. Then it happened; Robert popped the big question; he asked me to marry him.

There are many women who dream of being in my situation, marrying a wonderful, hard-working, caring, and God-fearing man. Yet, the entire time that I was planning the wedding, all I could do was worry. I literally worried myself sick and right into the hospital where I had to undergo bypass surgery. My left leg was cut open to remove veins to insert through my neck and into my chest. I was only 29 years old. Although doctors were able to discover the root cause of why I was losing blood flow to the left side of my body, I really believe that it was triggered by the level of stress and worry that I had brought upon myself. Even my doctor kept asking if I was under any type of stress that could have caused my condition to suddenly flair up and become life-threatening.

But what was I worried about? What had me so afraid?

I was stressed out because I was toting all of my past baggage right into my marriage. All of the hurt, pain, self-esteem issues, secrets, and lies were right there with me at the altar when I said "I do." Although my husband knew some things that I revealed in a state of drunkenness one night, he didn't know them all. I hadn't told him the whole truth about the past because I was afraid that if he found out he wouldn't want to be with me anymore. I just wanted us to hurry up and get married because I thought that marriage would fix everything, and I would be able to live happily ever after. I soon learned that marriage doesn't fix anything. Marriage didn't repair my broken heart and wounded soul. I quickly discovered the truth about the lie that many people spend their entire lives believing; a boy or a girl or a man or a woman will make everything okay. This is nothing but a lie!

Within days of getting married, I collapsed into a deep depression. I found myself constantly at war in my mind, especially when I was at home by myself. I had never been alone before. I had a roommate in college, and when I stayed with my mother someone was always around. So when my husband would leave for work or just be out for the day, I was forced to be by myself. Being alone with yourself can be a frightening experience if you don't know who you are. I began to think about things that I didn't want to think about and face the truth about my past. It wasn't long before I stopped wanting to be with me, and I discovered that I didn't even like who I was!

After a short period of time, I began having anxiety and panic attacks, which got so bad I couldn't sit through a movie, I cried for hours at a time, and I jumped at every little sound. The sound of the phone ringing or a door opening or closing would send me half out of my mind. The only time I felt any sense of protection from my thoughts was when I was at church.

To stop the anxiety and panic attacks I just kept

busy. I started working 12, 14, or 16 hours every day. I didn't come up for air. I had to constantly be doing something; talking on the phone, eating, reading, driving, anything to keep myself occupied. That was the worst time ever for me, and I'm still recovering from it today. I now realize that keeping busy was just another symptom of the problem and not the solution.

Once again, to people on the outside everything was fine. I was dealing with it all quite well in front of my family, friends, co-workers, and neighbors. I simply fell back into the routine of pretending that everything was okay. People thought that I was living the fairytale life, yet that was far from the truth. There would be days that I was knotted up in a ball in our bed crying. *"Jesus, help me! Please, help me!"* I felt so bad inside. I felt like I was making my husband suffer and live out my past with me. I felt that he didn't deserve to go through what I was putting him through. I either stuffed myself with all sorts of cakes and cookies all day and night, or I didn't eat at all. I went from one extreme to another. I was concerned about my weight, my looks, my hair, everything. Worst of all, I didn't want to have sex anymore.

Yes, you read it right. I no longer wanted to have sex. I never imagined that I would ever have sexual problems. It was the least of my worries. However, soon after saying "I do," my mind and body shut down and said "I can't." One reason for this was that I was no longer intoxicating and drugging myself just to have sex. But without taking something to help boost my courage, I no longer felt like I performed well enough. Another reason for this is that my relationships with men had always been superficial. They were like scripted roles in a movie. The real Stephanie never made it to the set. I had been involved in role play for such a long time, but with my husband it was the real deal. I wasn't acting like I was in love; I was in love. I didn't need drugs or alcohol to help me out. My feelings were all genuine.

I wanted my husband to be happy with me and our sex life, but I was so overwhelmed with the shame and guilt of my past that I was having an extremely difficult time being intimate with him. I had carried the scars of life with me from one soul and set of sheets to the next, not thinking about my life, other people's lives, or how it would affect my future. I hadn't realized that I'd connected not only physically but also emotionally with the men in my past, and that I couldn't just wake up the next morning, forget about them, and think that my life would go on as if nothing ever happened. I suddenly felt used and abused. I thought of myself as tainted and spoiled meat. It had gotten so bad that any sexual image, including those on television or on a billboard, would make me cringe and have an anxiety attack. I didn't want to see any type of intimacy between people. Regardless of how innocent it was, it made me think of how innocent I wasn't.

I also couldn't seem to get rid of the images from the past. The images from old relationships and experiences just wouldn't go away. No matter how hard I tried, I couldn't shake them. I was constantly thinking about every foul and nasty thing that I had done. My thoughts were contaminated. I hadn't learned to cast down negative thoughts and take control of my imagination; thus, my own thoughts were tormenting me with fear.

I was constantly watching over my shoulder, hoping that someone from the past wouldn't suddenly appear. There were many times I would go out to dinner or to a movie with my husband, and I would be unable to concentrate or focus on our conversation. I was afraid that a blast from the past would come strolling through the door at any minute. I never bothered to change my cell phone number, so I sometimes panicked when it rang. I was hoping that it wasn't some guy from three years ago saying he had just came across my telephone number and decided to give me a call. I would feel relieved when the caller ID revealed that it was only my mother or sister.

I lived in this self-afflicted torture for quite some time. Either I couldn't sleep, or I slept all day and then considered myself a lazy bum. Either I couldn't eat, or I ate like a pig and then called myself fat and complained about my weight. Either I couldn't think straight, or my mind would race out of control. I would think I was going crazy and that I was a nut case. I couldn't stop worrying, panicking, and crying. I just couldn't take it anymore. I was losing my mind. I was losing control of everything. I had fallen apart, and it had to come to an end.

Longing for answers and a way to end the pain, I bowed my head in shame for the very last time. Sobbing uncontrollably I asked, "Lord, how did I get here? How did I get to this point?" It was at that moment that I surrendered to God and my journey to freedom and wholeness began. I was finally willing and ready to face my enemy head-on. God slowly began to reveal things to me about my past and how things had gotten so bad in the first place. In the beginning, I only thought about what went on during my teen years. I began to remember things that were said and done to me that molded and shaped parts of my life. However, that just wasn't enough. Focusing on my teen years alone didn't add up and didn't answer enough questions. Questions like, why was I having sex at only 13 years old? Why did I find it so easy to give my soul away, and why did I hate myself so much?

As time went on, I began to dig deeper. Gradually, God began to answer my questions by revealing things to me about my childhood. I started remembering things about a past that as far as I knew up until that point didn't exist. Slowly, it all started coming back to me, the hugs, the kisses, rough and dirty hands being thrust between my legs, the grinding on men's body parts, and the many things I experienced as a young girl, which at some point I began to enjoy and seek after as a teenager and young adult. I started remembering everything that happened to me, and I began to connect the dots from one year to the next. Eventually I was able to see how I reached the point of a complete breakdown.

Since this journey began I've spent most of my time getting to know God, nurturing my soul, and rebuilding my life. Once again, I'm just taking one day at a time. It has been an emotional and sometimes painful journey, but because I was willing to take the ride to freedom, I now know that I didn't just wake up one day and choose the life that I once lived. I had grown into it.

PART II

SEXUAL ABUSE: THE PLAIN AND SIMPLE TRUTH

Chapter Four

Who, What, When, Where, and Why?

Is Child Sexual Abuse Really That Big of a Problem?

Child sexual abuse and exploitation involves using a child for sexual purposes. Examples of child sexual abuse include fondling, inviting a child to touch or be touched sexually, intercourse, rape, incest, sodomy, exhibitionism, or involving a child in prostitution or pornography.

Statistics show that child sexual abuse occurs at an alarming rate. There are nearly 3 million reports of child abuse made annually. In 2003, there were 906,000 child abuse convictions. The rate of child abuse is estimated to be three times greater than is reported.

According to most reliable studies of child sexual abuse in the United States, as many as one in three girls and one in five boys will be sexually abused at some point in their childhood. That means that in a class of 100 people, as many as 20 to 30 were sexually abused as children[1].

Myths About Sexual Abuse

SEXUAL ABUSE VICTIMS ARE VIOLENT AND REBELLIOUS

All sexual abuse victims are not violent and rebellious. Some victims are the exact opposite. They become extremely friendly. Other victims become introverted; they are shy and reserved.

MY CHILD WOULD TELL ME

Eighty-eight percent of victims don't tell according to information from the American Psychological Association[2]. Oftentimes a child, especially children between the ages of four and six, do not understand what is happening to them, so as far as they are concerned, there's nothing for them to tell.

A FIVE OR SIX YEAR OLD UNDERSTANDS WHAT'S GOING ON

Initially most sexual abuse victims mistake the hugs, touches, and kisses as normal love and attention. They think Daddy or Mommy is just bathing them when he or she touches their private areas.

ONLY MEN SEXUALLY ABUSE CHILDREN

Women commit sexual abuse also. Women in our society are usually portrayed as victims, but they are the offenders as well. When women commit sexual abuse, they tend to be excused in some way. Society believes that they must've gone through something bad, but when men abuse children they are considered monsters, and people immediately want to throw them in jail.

Who Sexually Abuses Children?

Child sexual abuse is not just a problem of the Catholic Church. It goes on in every family. It crosses all borders, regardless of race, economic status, or social class. In recent years, the Catholic Church has taken a major hit in the media in regards to sexual abuse. In my opinion, they're being used as the scapegoat to avoid a travesty that's going on far more behind the closed doors of our homes than it is in church buildings.

We now have several nationwide sexual predator tracking systems where people can find registered sex offenders in their neighborhoods. There is nothing wrong with this. We have a right to know who our neighbors are so that we can make decisions on whether or not we want to live near them. But do we not realize that these registered sex offenders are human beings? Sex offenders are not a special group of people from some foreign land. We talk about them as if they're not human. We refer to them as *the registered sex offenders*. Have you ever thought about where the people responsible for tracking them are getting their information from? *The registered sex offenders* are our family members, friends, co-workers, and neighbors, so registering them on a website does nothing to solve the problem within our own families.

We are living amongst sexual predators and sex offenders in our homes, but rarely is a child warned to beware of their own parents, siblings, uncles, grandparents, or babysitters. The home is a sanctuary and the place where people feel protected from the ills of society. When they can't find peace in their own homes, it often begins to spill out in other areas of their lives. Some people begin to act out in violent and erratic behavior, often hurting themselves or others.

Over the past five years, there has been an abundance of cases in which convicted rapists and murderers have came forth to say that childhood sexual abuse has had a detrimental effect on their lives and contributed to their sudden rage of killing their families or groups of school children.

While the media went into a frenzy to capture the story, it seems that everyone completely ignored the fact that these men and women said, "Hey, someone broke my heart and abused me, and I never dealt with that. Now I'm taking it out on someone else." As usual, the issue of sexual abuse was never talked about.

Don't Count Anyone Out!

In about 90 percent of child sexual abuse cases, the child knows the person that commits the abuse. The abusers can be immediate or extended family members; such as parents, stepparents, siblings, grandparents, uncles, and aunts. They can be friends of the family, babysitters, sports coaches, teachers, or religious leaders[3]. Sexual abuse doesn't have to take place over a long period of time. It can be one quick offense that can change or ruin a person's life forever. Be careful with anyone who has close contact with your children.

- Ninety-seven percent are male who are on average 10 years older than their victims.

- Females are more often perpetrators in child-care settings, including babysitting.

- Brother-sister incest is the most common form of incest but not the most commonly reported[4].

Kissing Cousins: Do Children Abuse Other Children?[5]

- Up to 50 percent of those who sexually abuse children are under the age of 18.

- Twenty to 50 percent of adolescents who have sexually abused children were themselves victims of physical abuse and approximately 40 to 80 percent were victims of sexual abuse.

- Children who abuse others often have been victimized in some way themselves. Acknowledging and addressing the distress these children have already faced is a good way to help end this abusive cycle.

Are Your Parents Really Your Heroes?

Most of us recall at some point in our lives a teacher asking us to identify our heroes. "Who do you want to be like when you grow up?" Besides our favorite sports figure, actor and singer, many of us were quick to identify our parents as the ones we looked up to and wanted to be like. Unfortunately, parents are not always heroes. In fact, to some they're the boogie man beneath the bed or the monster in the closet. The parents take on the very characteristics of the stranger they've warned their children about. Parents tell us: *Don't ever let anyone touch you; scream as loud as you can; bite a plug out of them; scratch their eyes out, and kick them where it hurts.* So what's a child to do when it's Mommy or Daddy that they need protection from?

Usually when I go out to speak about sexual abuse I take a survey in which I ask three basic questions:

1. Have you ever been sexually abused?

2. If yes, who was your abuser?

3. Did you tell anyone?

Despite all that I've personally experienced, nothing prepared me for the number of people who would answer yes and then check the box next to mother and/or father. On one occasion, I went to speak to a group of teenage girls. Immediately afterwards a 17-year-old girl approached me with a look of emptiness in her eyes. She shared her deepest and darkest secret with me. Her parents had gotten divorced, and initially she stayed at home with her mother. But her mother began molesting her, so she moved in with her father. Not long after moving in with him, he started having sex with her. I was so vexed by her story that the following night I had to get counseling myself. I found myself on the altar gasping for air and crying a puddle of tears. "If God has called you to do this, then you're going to have to learn how to handle it. You can't get emotional and take it home with you," the minister advised me. I've since learned how to deal with these stories because they come one after another. "Mommy kissed me." "Daddy made me rub his thing." These stories are more common than you'd ever know.

• Abuse of daughters by fathers and stepfathers is the most common form of reported incest. Commonly, the mother is unavailable to the father and is usually chronically ill or depressed. The mother is often the victim of child abuse when young.

• Sexual abuse by stepfathers is five times higher than among natural fathers. The most common age for onset of abuse is 10.

• Abuse by females may be higher than reported due to younger children confusing sexual abuse with normal hygiene care, and adolescent males may not be trained to recognize sexual activity with an older female as a form of abuse[6].

You would think that if parents were to discover or suspect that their spouses were molesting the children, they would immediately pack up their bags and children and leave until that person received help. However, this is not always the case.

Chapter Five

Knowing Is Half The Battle

"When you have sex with someone, you are having sex with everyone they have had sex with for the last 10 years, and everyone they and their partners have had sex with for the last 10 years."
—C. Everett Koop, M.D., Former U.S. Surgeon General[7]

The following chart compares the number of sexual partners encountered to the total number of people exposed to, assuming each partner has had the same number of sexual partners as you have had.[8]

# of Sexual Partners	1	2	3	4	5	6	7	8	9	10	11	12
# of People Exposed to	1	3	7	15	31	63	127	225	511	1023	2047	4095

Common Signs of Sexual Abuse[8]

- Promiscuous behavior
- Alcohol abuse
- Anxiety
- Binge eating (stuffing oneself with a lot of food in one sitting)
- Busy mind (racing thoughts)
- Caretaking/excessively pleasing people
- Competitive nature
- Controlling behavior
- Depression
- Drug abuse
- Easily influenced by others, music, and television
- Emotional instability
- Envy/jealousy
- Excessive spending habits
- Fear
- Guilt
- Low self-esteem
- Poor self-image
- Sexual/lustful thoughts
- Sexually Transmitted Diseases (STD) Vaginal or rectal bleeding, pain, itching, swollen genitals, vaginal discharge (STDs can cause permanent or long-term gynecological effects such as vaginal

stretching, miscarriages, stillbirths, bladder infections, and infertility.)

- Suspicious mind (thinking that people always have ulterior motives)

- Uncomfortable around doctors of the opposite sex

Other Signs of Sexual Abuse

- Nightmares, trouble sleeping, fear of the dark, or other sleeping problems

- Extreme fear of "monsters" or the "boogie man"

- Spacing out at odd times

- Loss of appetite, trouble eating or swallowing

- Sudden mood swings: rage, fear, anger, or withdrawal

- Fear of certain people or places (e.g., a child may not want to be left alone with a babysitter, a friend, a relative, or some other child or adult, or a child who is usually talkative and cheery may become quiet and distant when around a certain person.)

- Stomach illness all of the time with no identifiable reason

- An older child behaving like a younger child, such as bed-wetting or thumb sucking

- Sexual activities with toys or other children, such as simulating sex with dolls or asking other children/siblings to behave sexually

- New words for private body parts

- Refusing to talk about a "secret" he/she has with an adult or older child
- Talking about a new older friend
- Suddenly having money
- Cutting or burning oneself as an adolescent
- Flirtatious behavior:

Flirtatious behavior is not something you'll find listed in many studies on sexual abuse. I once had very flirtatious behavior. It came out in the way that I said hello, smiled at men, shook hands, and made eye contact with them. After I got married, my husband brought this to my attention. I was furious with him at first. I thought he was being overly sensitive, but then I made it a point to be more conscious of my behavior and how I interacted with other men, and I found out that he was right. It wasn't intentional, but flirting was something that came naturally to me. It was learned behavior and a habit that I had picked up as a child. As soon as I realized that I had a flirting problem, I put a stop to it. I've heard many people say there's nothing wrong with a little flirting here and there, but I'm a married woman, and there was no need opening a door if I had no intentions of allowing someone to walk through it.

What To Watch For When Adults Are With Children

If you witness a child and an adult interacting and it makes you uncomfortable, don't dismiss it as paranoia. Don't worry about overreacting. It's better to be safe than sorry. Following is a list of signs to look out for when adults are around children.

WATCH FOR AN ADULT OR OLDER CHILD WHO[9]:

• Refuses to let a child set any of his or her own limits.

• Insists on hugging, touching, kissing, tickling, wrestling with or holding a child even when the child does not want this affection.

• Is overly interested in the sexuality of a particular child or teen (e.g., talks repeatedly about the child's developing body or interferes with normal teen dating).

• Manages to get time alone or insists on time alone with a child with no interruptions.

• Spends most of his/her spare time with children and has little interest in spending time with someone his/her own age.

• Regularly offers to babysit many different children for free or takes children on overnight outings alone.

• Buys children expensive gifts or gives them money for no apparent reason.

• Frequently walks in on children/teens in the bathroom.

- Allows children or teens to consistently get away with inappropriate behaviors.

OTHER SIGNS TO LOOK FOR:

- The child or adult has a startled look or stunned reaction when other people enter the room.

- Unusual quietness when conversation should be heard.

- Unexplained time lapses of activity when you ask a child what they have been doing (Do they always answer, "Nothing?").

- Adults who do not take interest in dating people their own age.

Chapter Six

Protecting the Ones You Love

How To Prevent Sexual Abuse

There are some things that people often don't recognize or they overlook because it comes across as normal behavior, or it seems too far-fetched to be true. Keep in mind that I speak to you from experience and not research alone.

First, I do realize that we have to allow children to be children. I also recognize that at some point children become curious about kissing and about their body parts, but this is not an excuse for children to act out adult sexual behavior. This is when parents should be extremely cautious about how much freedom they give their children and where and with whom they allow their kids to spend time. Parents need to think twice before they send their kids off to the babysitter, in the back room to play with the other kids, outside to play with their friends, or over Auntie Jane's or Uncle John's house to spend the night.

Childhood Sex Games

Because child on child sexual abuse is often how molestation begins in the first place, we must begin with trying to prevent the cycle from repeating itself with our children.

➤ "HIDE-AND-GO-GET'M"

You're it! You know how the game goes. The person who gets tagged "it" closes his or her eyes and counts to 20 while everyone else scatters to find the perfect hiding place: under a car, behind a tree, or in a neighbor's garage. Whomever "it" finds first becomes his or her mate for a quick kissing and groping session. That person then takes his or her place as "it," and the counting starts all over again. The game is usually played with a group of boys and girls who team up and play against each other. Usually by the end of the game, everyone has had the opportunity to kiss and grope one another.

While conducting research for this topic, my husband asked me if children still played this game because we rarely see kids outside playing anymore. A quick phone call to a group of kids ages 9, 11, and 16 confirmed what I thought. Although kids today are not as active outdoors as they were when I was growing up, they're still playing the X-rated version of Hide-and-Seek.

➤ "DOCTOR! DOCTOR! CHECK MY HEARTBEAT!"

This game is played quite innocently among a lot of children who are merely showing their fascination with this profession, but sometimes playing "Doctor" loses its innocence and becomes a way for kids to act out sexually toward one another. CPR turns into tongue kissing and checking blood pressure and heartbeats is just another way for kids to touch each other's bodies.

➤ "WHEN A HOUSE IS NOT A HOME"

"Let's play House!" I heard this many times growing

up, and it's still one of the most popular home games today, especially when groups of kids spend the night together. Someone takes on the role of mother and father, and the other kids become their children. If there are enough kids around, then the roles of uncle, aunt, boyfriend and girlfriend may be added. The game is basically centered on the kids following the parents' rules and being spanked and punished for being disobedient. However, this game allows for a lot of sexual interaction between the "parents" and other children acting as the adult couples. The most sexual interaction takes place when the children are ordered to bed for doing something mischievous, such as not doing their homework or skipping class.

> ## "SPIN THE BOTTLE"

I was shocked to hear that people are still playing "Spin the Bottle." Just in case someone isn't familiar with this game, here's a quick overview: a group of people get together and spin a bottle and whomever the bottle points to must kiss the spinner. I was shocked because I hadn't heard about it in such a long time. However, I was more shocked because it was an 11-year-old girl who yelled out "Spin the Bottle" when I asked what games kids play in which they do bad things.

> ## "SEVEN MINUTES IN HEAVEN"

"Seven Minutes in Heaven" is a game that's new to me. It's actually quite simple. The group chooses a leader, who is usually the oldest or most popular kid in the group. The leader then chooses two other children who have to kiss for seven minutes. I don't know if I was more shocked by the game itself or by the fact that kids were kissing for seven minutes. I thought, *Wow! Seven whole minutes of kissing, and they actually time each other.*

Know What's Going On In Your Child's Life

Oftentimes, children are molested because of their parents' negligence. There are parents who spend more time at parties and away from home than they do with their children, and I'm not speaking of those who work or attend school. Too often the children find themselves left at home alone or always over someone else's house spending the night. Parents must realize that when they don't spend quality time with their children, they are leaving the children to figure out life on their own. Many parents don't know what's going on in their children's lives, who their friends and teachers are, where they spend their time, or what they watch on TV and listen to on the radio. If parents paid more attention to these things, they might recognize that something is not right in their children's lives. When children don't receive love from their parents, they will seek it from someone else. This makes children easy targets for abusers.

Spending The Night

The number of places children should be allowed to spend the night should be minimal and in some cases, zero. This includes homes of family members and close friends. Although parents may keep a close watch on their children at home, they can't possibly know everything that's going on behind someone else's doors. I wasn't always at home when I was being taken advantage of. Much of the abuse I experienced happened while visiting other family members or friends of the family. I come from a large family, and it was common for me to spend weekends at one of my relative's homes.

You might be thinking that your parents, brothers, or sisters would never harm your children, but when it comes to sexual abuse, you can't remove anyone from the equation. Besides, there may even be a situation where it's not the adults living in the home that are committing the abuse. It might be a guest. It was never my parents who abused me. It was always other people living with us or visiting our home. This means that every child who spent the night at our home during the years that I was being molested was a potential victim. Also consider that it may be other children living in the home who are the offenders. Statistics show that sexually abused children often share their experiences with other children their age or younger.

On the subject of allowing children to spend the night at other people's homes, I find it disturbing when parents know the circumstances at a family member's or friend's home and still allow their children to visit. They don't allow their children to watch R- or X-rated movies, listen to profane and degrading music, or use profanity while at home, but will allow them to visit homes where they know these things are taking place. Why a mother would allow her sister or girlfriend to babysit her children when every other week there's a different man with his feet propped up on her coffee table just doesn't make sense.

Daycare Centers, Babysitters, and Cohabitation

It is my belief that children of single parents may be more vulnerable to sexual abuse. I believe this because of the need for babysitters and daycare providers. Because single parents are the primary caregivers and usually work outside of the home, their children spend a lot of time in the care of family, friends, and strangers. I also believe this because single parents often share living space with relatives or friends to cut back on living expenses or to avoid living alone. Therefore, their children find themselves sharing living space with people other than their parents and siblings. Sometimes the children share bedrooms with other children who have been exposed to molestation, who then introduce them to the abuse.

SEXUAL ABUSE AND DAYCARE CENTERS[10]

- An average of 5.5 children per 10,000 enrolled in daycare is sexually abused.

- A survey of sex offenders involved in daycare center abuse revealed that 45 percent were between the ages of 12 and 17 and 28 percent were between the ages of 18 and 24.

- Forcible fondling accounts for approximately 42 percent of sexual abuse cases.

- Forcible sodomy (unnatural acts, deviant sex, intercourse, oral sex, anal sex) accounts for approximately 11 percent of daycare cases.

- Children under age six, the group most likely to be cared for by babysitters, are also the most likely to be victimized by them.

> ➤ **HOW DO YOU MINIMIZE THE RISK OF SEXUAL ABUSE FOR YOUR CHILDREN IN A DAYCARE SETTING?**

1. Don't select a daycare center just because it is close to your home. If you have to wake up 10 to 30 minutes earlier to drive your children to a daycare provider that's farther away, then do so. Ten or 30 minutes can make a difference in your child's life.

2. Screen daycare providers. Do a background check for prior criminal histories.

3. Get the provider's basic information (name, address, telephone number, Social Security Number, and educational background).

4. Have a list of all personnel working in the center, and research these individuals as well.

5. Get references from trusted family members and friends.

6. Conduct an interview with them personally; try to gain an impression of the attitude and temperament.

7. Do a thorough check on the facilities: cleanliness, food stock, basic necessities such as toilet tissue, soap, and toys.

8. Do random and unannounced visits.

9. Check books, pictures, and T.V. programs children are exposed to.

DATING AND GOING OUT

Dating and going out is a controversial issue. But we must recognize the difference between the two. Some people are dating, seeing one person, with the intention of developing a relationship with that person, while other people are just going out; they are keeping their options open and are seeing several people. Regardless of what the person calls the relationship, the individuals they're involved with shouldn't be allowed around the children until the two people are convinced that they are right for one another. Honestly, it's very difficult to know much about another person after going out for a few weeks or even a couple of months. I've spoken with many young ladies over the past several years who have confessed to being sexually abused by their mothers' boyfriends. Consider this scenario for the woman who is simply going out:

It's 1 A.M., and the mother is sound asleep. Her boyfriend, whom she's being seeing for two months, slips out of bed to go to the bathroom only to find his way to her nine-year-old daughter's bedroom. After molesting her, robbing her of her innocence, and threatening her life, he quietly tiptoes back into the mother's bedroom, climbs back into the bed and wraps himself around the mother as if nothing ever happened. In the meantime, the daughter is in her room staring at the walls trying to figure out what just happened to her and what she did to deserve it. The little girl did nothing to deserve it; unfortunately, the mother made an unwise decision by giving a man she barely knew access to her child. I have family members and close friends who have never stepped foot in my home. Likewise, if I were a single mom, I would never allow a man I've known for two months inside my home around my children.

Be Careful What You Let Your Children Watch and Listen To

In studies of juvenile offenders, younger perpetrators tend to abuse younger victims, but are more likely to have intercourse with older victims. Sex acts by young children, between young children, are a learned behavior and are associated with sexual abuse or exposure to adult sex or pornography[11].

I remember watching a popular movie back in the early '90s. I was around 17 years old. There was a scene in which two actors were engaged in sex. The man was so satisfied with how the woman performed in bed and how she made him feel, that he practically gave up his entire life as he knew it just to be with her. I remember thinking at that very moment: *I want to make a man feel that way.* I played that scene out in my head many times throughout the years.

Sure, this may sound silly to some folks, but people, especially children, often try to imitate something or someone they see in the media or hear in a song. I witnessed this while visiting one of the local high schools. There's a song that talks about tossing money up in the air on women in topless bars. The song is totally degrading to women, yet a young girl around 15 years old was singing and bouncing to the nasty lyrics. It was a disturbing scene. I also witnessed a sickening incident involving 5 little girls between the ages of 6 and 13. While visiting my mother, the little girls who live on her block were outside dancing to a song that was all about them "getting their freak on." The young girls were dancing, popping, and grinding to the voice of a very popular female artist. The youngest girl laid down on the ground, opened her legs, and began rotating them in a butterfly motion.

We must be careful about what we let our children see and hear. If they become used to hearing and seeing these types of messages and images, their curiosity is piqued even more, and this makes it easier for someone to lure them into a relationship of sexual abuse.

Talk To Your Children!

Parents have a responsibility to protect their children as much as they can. This includes talking to children and being honest with them. Children need to understand that sometimes even the people they love and care about can do bad things. This shouldn't be a one-time conversation. It should be a conversation that's revisited throughout the years, especially between the ages of 5 and 13 when children are most vulnerable to sexual abuse. Parents must say more than, "Don't let anyone touch you." They must help children understand that anyone consists of everyone: mom, dad, brothers, sisters, aunts, uncles, neighbors, grandparents, teachers, cousins, pastors, camp counselors, and other children.

Chapter Seven

The Secret

Why Don't People Tell

According to the Merriam-Webster Dictionary, a secret is something that is hidden or kept from general knowledge. Throughout the past two decades, people have been more willing than ever to share their safely-kept secrets with the world, especially about AIDS, homosexuality, drug usage, promiscuity, and lives of infidelity. Things that were once considered taboo and immoral are now out in the open and spread out over books, television, newspapers, and tabloid magazines for the whole world to see. When it comes to child sexual abuse and molestation, however, no one is talking. People don't want to talk about it because they don't want other people to know that it's going on in their families. The truth of the matter is that it's going on in every family. It may not be happening in your family today, but rest assured that someone in your family has been sexually abused.

"Why don't people tell?" is a question that could never be answered with just one response. Chances are, if you were to poll just 10 victims you might get at least 30 different answers. There is no such thing as "the answer." Sexual abuse victims usually have several different reasons why they don't tell, which can range from fear to shame.

Before we talk about why victims don't tell, let's address the issue of why other people don't tell. When I say "other people," I'm talking about those people who are not victims but are very much aware of what's going on and choose to not do or say anything. Have you ever suspected that a child you know was being abused? Did you report it?

I was talking to a family member about the abuse I experienced, and it seemed like my heart stopped beating for a full minute; the person told me that they knew about it a long time ago; they had walked in on another girl in my family being sexually abused. They chose not to say anything because at the time they felt as if they were protecting our family.

Too often, signs and suspicions of sexual abuse go ignored and unreported. People do not report sexual abuse for various reasons. It's only after things go terribly wrong and something bad happens to the child that you hear friends, teachers, neighbors, and other family members say that they knew something didn't seem right a long time ago. Not only have surveys shown that people don't report suspected abuse, but many admit to witnessing it and doing nothing about it.

The reasons for not reporting abuse include not

knowing where to call and misconceptions regarding what will happen once a report of known or suspected abuse is made to the police or a child protective services agency. Many people incorrectly believe that:

- **MYTH**: By law, abused children must be removed from their homes immediately.

    o **FACT**: This is the least likely outcome. Surprisingly, children are rarely permanently removed from the home. Some are taken away upon completion of a full investigation.

- **MYTH**: Child abuse cannot be reported anonymously.

    o **FACT**: In most states, you don't need to provide your name.

- **MYTH**: The person reported for the abuse is entitled to know who made the report.

    o **FACT**: Authorities do not have to reveal their sources.

OTHER REASONS ABUSE GOES UNREPORTED

- People believe it's not their problem because it's not their child.

- People believe it's not their business to get involved.

- People don't want to bring shame and embarrassment to their families or friends.

- People fear being physically harmed by the abuser.

- People fear the division of their families.

Why Do Parents Deny Sexual Abuse?

Parents deny that the abuse happened for many reasons, including shame and embarrassment. They are ashamed of the fact that they allowed the abuse to go on without doing anything about it. It's like saying, "I choose this man or woman over the safety and well-being of my child." Admitting that they chose to do nothing about the abuse puts them at risk for having to suffer legal ramifications and being ridiculed by their family and friends. Even if it's true, people don't want to hear or be accused of turning their backs on their own children. Thus, denial becomes the easiest way for them to deal with it.

You may hear some parents say, "Well, I wasn't 100 percent sure that it was happening. I suspected that something was going on, but I just wasn't sure. My child never told me anything, so I thought it was just my imagination or my being overly protective. I didn't want to create a problem where one didn't exist." If parents even suspect that someone is doing something to their children, they should act on it immediately. Again, it is the parents' responsibility to protect their children at all times. They cannot afford to worry about hurting someone's feelings at the expense of their children. Yes, they need to act with caution, be led by God and not their emotions, but they must not sit back and do nothing.

OTHER REASONS PARENTS DENY SEXUAL ABUSE

- **FEAR**: It is often the number one reason why people make many of the choices they do in life.
  - o People fear their spouse or family member going to jail.
  - o People are afraid of having their children removed from the home by the police or child protective services.
  - o People are afraid of being attacked and harmed by the abuser.

- **LONELINESS**: They don't want the relationship or marriage to end.

- **FINANCIAL SECURITY**: Some parents fear the inability to financially provide for their children upon a possible divorce or separation.

- **SELFISHNESS**: Some people are self-centered. They only consider themselves and the consequences that telling would have on their lives.

- **LACK OF KNOWLEDGE**: They didn't know that it was a crime. Most people, including sexual abuse victims, don't even recognize or acknowledge that a crime has been committed against them or their children. Some victims believe that because the abuser was a family member, it doesn't count as a crime.

I recall discussing this very topic with a family member who was also sexually abused. Interestingly, she said that she had never thought of it as a crime or considered herself a victim. She described it as "something that just happened to me." I needed her to understand exactly what happened to her, so I asked her to consider the following scenario:

What if your five-year-old daughter was outside playing, and a neighbor, whether teenager or adult, snatched her into his home and sexually abused her? He rubbed between her legs, kissed her affectionately, stuck his tongue down her throat, made her have oral sex with him, and had her fondle him until he had an orgasm. How would you feel? What would you do?

She calmly said, "I would kill that ___."

"So what's the difference when someone in the family does it?" I asked. She just sat silent for a long time.

Why Didn't I Tell?

As I stated in the very beginning, I honestly can't recall what I was thinking at five and six years old. For that time period, I can only give you my opinion. However, I do know why I didn't tell once I got older, so that's where I'll begin.

I LIKED IT!

It felt good, and I didn't want it to stop. Research has shown that people are born sensual and sexual beings. Even at the age of two, children recognize when a touch on certain body parts makes them feel good. Since I had been sexually abused for so long, I grew to love what it felt like when my body was touched. By the time I was 10, I didn't want it to end. Those who abused me no longer had to woo me into it because I went looking for it. I had become totally infatuated with one of my molesters, sometimes finding myself jealous and envious of the girls he brought around.

It's important to understand that the flesh doesn't recognize names and faces. It reacts to physical desire, and what was happening to my flesh felt good to me. Isn't that why most people have sex in the first place, because it feels good? The body is separate from the soul. Your head might be thinking I really hate this person, but the body is not saying that. It doesn't know the difference between people. A touch is a touch is a touch. Someone can touch you, and it may make you sick to your stomach because of who it is and what's taking place, but it doesn't mean that it doesn't feel good to the flesh. Unfortunately, between the ages of 5 and 18 when people are sexually abused, the body tends to have more control over the mind.

GUILT

I didn't feel guilty as a young child. I knew that it wasn't right, but I don't think I even recognized the seriousness of the situation. I was only five years old. Feeling guilty about being involved in sexual acts shouldn't be a five-year-old child's problem. Once I was older and realized how serious it was, I felt guilty about it. I was disappointed in myself. I thought *what type of person would do what I was doing? What type of person am I?*

FEAR

I thought something bad would happen to me. I thought my parents would punish me. There was also the fear of being taken away from my parents and being sent to live in a juvenile or girls' home, what we called being *caught up in the system.* I had heard the words *Child Protective Services* many times growing up. Kids in my family and neighborhood were always threatening to call them up on their parents, to which most parents replied, "Go ahead! Call them! Better yet, let me call them for you." I knew that Child Protective Services was real, and I wasn't trying to go there. Therefore, regardless of how bad the situation was at home, telling just wasn't an option for me.

Not only did I fear what could happen to me, but I feared what might happen to my abusers. I loved most of these people, and I didn't want them to get in trouble. I didn't want anyone to go to jail. I didn't want anyone to die either, and one thing I knew for sure is that if my father found out, someone would have ended up dead or in jail. I didn't want my family to fall apart. I definitely didn't want anyone mad at me. I was always told that families stick together through thick and thin. *You don't allow anything to break up the family.*

SHAME

Shame is different from guilt. It's not about being right or wrong, but how one feels internally about his or her actions. Many people do things knowing that it's wrong, but they don't necessarily feel bad about it.

At some point I knew that it was wrong, and I felt bad about it. It was such a horrible feeling knowing that I had kissed and did these things with people in my own family. I felt nasty and disgusting. Sometimes I wished that I could scrub it all away with some soap and water, but that wouldn't do it. I couldn't help but wonder what others would think of me and the embarrassment it would bring to my family.

> *"Fear not; for thou shalt not be ashamed: neither be thou confounded; for thou shalt not be put to shame: for thou shalt forget the shame of thy youth, and shalt not remember the reproach of thy widowhood any more."*
> —Isaiah 54:4

Other Reasons the Abused Don't Tell

- **PARENTS DON'T BELIEVE THE CHILD:** Some kids try to tell their parents and are not believed. Some parents get angry at their children. These kids have a hard time. Their feelings of betrayal are enormous.

- **FEAR:** Some children are told that they will go to jail if they tell because they are as guilty as the offender.

- **THREATS OF HARM:** I don't ever remember being threatened by any of my abusers, nor do I recall any threats against other family members. However, many victims report being threatened by their abusers. Not only do they threaten their lives, but the lives of the ones they love, most often a sibling or parent.

- **SEDUCTION:** The very thought of a grown man or woman seducing a child can make you want to gag, but it's surprising to what extent some people will go to satisfy their sexual lusts. I was seduced by kind words, sweet affection, and gifts. All children like to be told how beautiful, sweet, and nice they are. Sometimes those kind words are no more than sweet nothings to lure in a child. The affection shown through pinches on the cheeks, bear hugs, and little pecks on the mouth can be cover-ups for what's to come. Adults buying children an unusual amount of gifts can be another sign. All kids like gifts. Adults like gifts. But we all know that a stick of bubble gum and a pack of Now and Later candy can go a long way with a small child. Imagine how far a person can get with a child when the candy turns into money, trendy clothes, and shoes.

- **LACK OF UNDERSTANDING:** Whether it's out of fear, denial, or plain irresponsibility, some parents never take the time to talk to their children about sexual abuse, and others avoid going into much detail. They tell their children, "Don't ever let anyone touch you," or "Tell me if someone touches you." That, however, is not enough. First of all, children need clarity on the title "*anyone.*" They need to understand that "anyone" includes Mom, Dad, uncles, aunts, sisters, brothers, babysitters, teachers, friends, or strangers. Secondly, "Don't let anyone touch you" is such a vague statement to make to a young child. Most young children have no idea what a sexual touch is, so when Uncle Ken picks up little Ebony and strokes her back or pats her bottom, chances are she doesn't recognize it as a sexual touch. Besides, she sees him as her Uncle Ken, the one who loves her and buys her candy. How about when Uncle John fondles little Christopher's penis? At six years old, little Christopher has likely never seen sex before, and his parents haven't had the bird and bees talk with him yet. Therefore, he doesn't know what's going on. Next thing, little Christopher is nine years old and having oral sex with a grown man.

- **FAMILY LOYALTY:** Don't ever put your business in the streets. What goes on at home stays at home.

- **ERRONEOUS TEACHING:** We are taught that people who pose any type of danger or threat are bad people, the boogie man, and strangers. Therefore, our families and the ones we love do not count.

- **ERRONEOUS THINKING:** People often think, *"It happened a long time ago. I'll get over it. Anyway, there's nothing that I can do about it now."*

- **ADMIRATION:** Having a high regard for the offender can keep the abused silent. Naturally, no one wants to bring shame upon someone he or she looks up to.

Chapter Eight

Families Under Siege—
Consequences of Sexual Abuse

Homosexuality and Lesbianism

This book primarily focuses on the effects of sexual abuse on girls, but I can't leave out the young men as if it doesn't happen to them also. Statistics reveal that as many as 1 out of 5 young men are molested. Many of my family members dismiss one of my male cousin's erratic behaviors as his being crazy; he roams the streets homeless and talks to himself all day. He may be mentally ill now, but he wasn't always this way. He was once a normal young man who liked basketball, football, fast cars, and video games just like most other boys. Whenever I happen to run into him on the streets or he comes to the neighborhood, I listen to the things he mumbles. In between his pleas for money and food, I've heard stories of him being sexually abused as a child. It must be difficult for a boy to grow up and feel like a man when his first sexual experience was with another man.

Many of these male victims begin to question their masculinity. While homosexuality is a choice that many men make, at ages five and six, these young victims were not given a choice. It was forced upon them. This same rule applies to women. A lot of the young girls that I speak to who are involved in lesbian relationships often admit that they were molested by other women, including their mothers. Some say that because of the abuse, they always felt that they were somehow different from other girls.

Perhaps the most tragic aspect of the homosexual-pedophile connection is the fact that men who sexually molest boys all too often lead their victims into homosexuality and pedophilia. The evidence indicates that a high percentage of homosexuals and pedophiles were themselves sexually abused as children. The *Archives of Sexual Behavior* reports:

One of the most salient findings of this study is that 46 percent of homosexual men and 22 percent of homosexual women reported having been molested by a person of the same gender.

Noted child sex abuse expert David Finkelhor found that *boys victimized by older men were over four times more likely to be currently engaged in homosexual activity than were non-victims.*

The finding applied to nearly half the boys who had had such an experience. Further, the adolescents themselves often linked their homosexuality to their sexual victimization experiences[12].

A study of 394 self-identified bisexual and homo-sexual adolescents in the 7th to 12th grades revealed:

- The proportion of younger respondents (defined as 14 years of age or younger) with a history of sexual abuse was almost four times greater among girls (14.9 percent) than boys (4.1 percent).

- None of the younger boys and 42.1 percent of the younger girls who reported a history of sexual abuse discussed the abuse with someone.

- More than 30 percent of older girls (defined as 15 years of age or older) compared to 16.7 percent of older boys reported a history of sexual abuse.

- More than 54 percent of older boys and 45.8 percent of older girls who reported a history of sexual abuse had never discussed the abuse with anyone.

Generational Sex Offenders

One-third of abused and neglected children will eventually victimize their own children or someone else's children, thus perpetuating a generational cycle of abuse.

Gateway To Other Destructive Behaviors[13]

- Children who have been sexually abused are 2.5 times more likely develop alcohol abuse.

- Children who have been sexually abused are 3.8 times more likely develop drug addictions.

- Nearly two-thirds of the people in treatment for drug abuse reported being abused as children.

- Eighty percent of young adults who had been abused met the diagnostic criteria for at least one psychiatric disorder by the age 21, including depression, anxiety, eating disorders, and post-traumatic stress disorder.

- Abused children are 25 percent more likely to experience teen pregnancy.

- Children who experience child abuse and neglect are 59 percent more likely to be arrested as a juvenile, 28 percent more likely to be arrested as an adult, and 30 percent more likely to commit violent crimes.

- Abused teens are three times less likely to practice safe sex, putting them at greater risk for STDs and AIDS.

- More than 14 percent of all men in prison in the USA were abused as children.

- More than 36 percent of all women in prison were abused as children[14].

Fear and Lack of Trust

Many people who are sexually abused fear trusting other people. This should come as no surprise considering they couldn't trust the people who should have been protecting and caring for them as children. Hurt by men at an early age, some women feel that all men are untrustworthy and will hurt them in some way or another. There was a time in my own life that I didn't even trust male doctors. I thought that even they had ulterior motives.

Some women are also taught when they are young that all men are dogs. With this embedded deep in their hearts, coupled with the experience of being sexually abused by the men they love, they believe that men are supposed to treat them poorly. Some find it difficult to settle into relationships because of this attitude and lack of trust. I remember feeling as if every man whom I knew loved me ended up leaving me, including two of my uncles and my grandfather, all of whom died before my 25th birthday. I just expected men to dishonor me, cheat on me, and leave me. I thought that was just how men were. Whether they died or just got up and walked out, in my heart I never thought they would be around for long.

Because of my own lack of trust and fear issues, every time my husband would leave home I would say, "I love you." However, it wasn't always out of the sincerity of my heart. Although I do love him, I was telling him this so often based on fear, fear that it would be the last time I would see him. I was afraid that something would happen to him, and he wouldn't return home. That fear was tormenting!

I was also dealing with a completely different type of fear and trust issue that women rarely talk about. Unlike the common mistrust issue of infidelity, I wasn't afraid that my husband would cheat on me because he saw another pretty face or nice body. Instead, I was jealous of his male friends. Some of them I wanted to make disappear, especially his single friends. It didn't matter that my husband had never given me any reason not to trust him, I just didn't want those single brothers trying to tempt him into doing something he didn't have any business doing. Honestly, I was thinking about a lot of the single people that I knew, those who don't like to see other people happy and would try anything to sabotage someone else's relationship. Yes, this was a personal issue that only I could deal with, but I'm sure it's something that other women who have fear and trust issues experience.

Teenage Pregnancy and Prostitution

Teen pregnancy is a widespread concern for thousands across the world. Sexual abuse is the leading cause of extremely young pregnancies. Rare cases involve actual intercourse with acquaintances from locations such as school, but most are the result of molestation. This comes in the form of incest and rape[15].

➤ CHELSEA'S STORY: A FAST LITTLE GIRL

Five-year-old Chelsea was molested by her older brother Mark, who was 12. The abuse went on until she was eight years old. Once Mark became interested in older girls, he stopped bothering her. But when it stopped, Chelsea missed the attention and the way it made her feel. Therefore, she didn't try to stop it or tell anyone when her 26-year-old uncle started molesting her.

It began on a Saturday night when her mother had to work late and sent her over to her uncle's house for him to babysit. The sexual abuse went on for five years and Chelsea, as she promised her brother and uncle, never told a soul.

When Chelsea turned 13, she began to go through puberty and her body started maturing. She had already experienced both orgasms and oral sex, and her menstrual cycle had also begun.

Because Chelsea was 13, her mother really didn't see the need to have anyone babysit her anymore, so she stayed at home alone while her mother worked two jobs. Her brother Mark, who was 20 years old, was still living at home. He had a lot of male friends between the ages of 20 and 25 who often stopped by to visit him. Chelsea saw the way they looked at and admired her growing body. She liked the attention. She was used to getting this type of attention from older men, having gotten it from her brother and uncle for eight years.

When Chelsea turned 15 years old, one of her brother's friends stopped by the house when Mark wasn't home. Chelsea and the young man became engaged in a conversation, which ultimately led to her skipping school and sneaking over to his house.

Although he didn't have any contact with her outside of the confinement of his bedroom, she considered him her boyfriend. She was excited about having an older man in her life. They were having sex regularly and not using condoms. He told her that he loved her and because he was her first, he trusted her, so they didn't need to use the condoms. Chelsea got pregnant. Too young to get an abortion on her own, which is what both of them really wanted, she had the child, a beautiful baby girl with soft hair and gorgeous eyes. Chelsea saw her as a little princess with the whole world in front of her. She named her Nina.

When Chelsea turned 16, her mother became frustrated with the financial burden she was experiencing. She couldn't afford a regular babysitter for her own children, so she definitely couldn't afford one for Nina, who she suddenly had to feed, clothe, and care for. So, Chelsea dropped out of school to take care of the baby while her mother worked during the day.

Still a little girl herself, Chelsea hung out with her friends at night while her mother kept the baby. As expected, the relationship with her brother's friend had gone sour, and he was nowhere to be found. So as teenagers often do, she found herself in and out of relationships with different guys. Most of them were much older than she. They introduced her to alcohol and drugs, which she enjoyed because they helped her to avoid the way she was feeling about her messed-up life.

Chelsea's mother began to get on her case about hanging out and not helping her care for the baby. Her mother was not happy with her daughter's lifestyle and blamed it all on Chelsea for always having been a "fast little girl." The arguments led to physical altercations, so eventually her mother put her out.

What happened next is what happens in the lives of many of our beautiful, young women; Chelsea began exotic dancing in a club and prostituting herself in order to provide for herself and her child. She also moved in with a friend who didn't mind her living with her, but was not up for babysitting someone else's kids. She had her own three kids to watch.

In order to keep working, Chelsea sent little Nina over to Mark's house every night. She had forgotten about how he sexually abused her for years. Besides, it happened years ago when they were kids. However, Mark had never received any type of help or counseling for his problem and began to molest little Nina, and the cycle repeated itself all over again. Years later Nina found herself in the same situation as her mother.

This may be a fabricated story created just to prove a point, but for many abuse victims it is real. The generational cycle of abuse leads to other generational problems within a family.

According to noted expert Dorothy M. Neddermeyer, PhD[16]:

* Of teenage, unwed mothers, 60-67 percent were incest survivors.

* Ninety-six percent of teenage prostitutes were sexually molested in childhood. Almost 80 percent had become prostitutes before age 18.

* Sixty percent of prostitutes were 16 or under; many were younger than 13.

One year, while attending a fundraising dinner, I had the pleasure of meeting Ms. Robbie Haynes, Founder of the Women of Virtue Development Institute (WOVDI). Not long after we met, she phoned me to talk about her desire to help teenage girls, specifically in the area of teenage pregnancy. Here is a woman whom I barely knew, yet I found myself sharing my deepest secret with her. "If you want to cut down on teenage pregnancy, you must address the issue of child sexual abuse and molestation," I told her. "No one could tell me not to have sex at 13 years old. I wanted to have sex. It was all that I knew. I had been taught about sex since I was kid, and I didn't want to stop. I didn't want to be a virgin," I continued. That conversation changed my life forever and began the work that I do today.

The following spring Robbie asked me to speak at a conference that she was hosting for 200 teen girls, and I agreed. Of course, that meant that I had to tell my mother about the abuse, which I did the night before the conference. The first time I ever spoke publicly about the abuse was in front of over 200 people. Almost everyone in the room was in tears, including me. After the conference ended, I spent hours talking to young girls and older women about their own experiences. Having the opportunity to talk to those young ladies proved that I was right; a great majority of our young girls are having sex and becoming pregnant because of their experience with sexual abuse at a young age. "Chelsea" represents thousands of young girls around the world. I then began speaking as much as I could in schools, churches, private home meetings, wherever anyone would let me tell my story.

PART III

INTERVIEWS AND FREQUENTLY ASKED QUESTIONS

(HIGHLY SENSITIVE INFORMATION)

Chapter Nine

Violated—Lisa & Elizabeth

*"I was touched, probed, and forced for
seven years to make my stepfather feel
good. I had semen shot in my mouth more
times than I can number."*

Lisa's* Story

Q: Who was your abuser, and what is your relationship like with that person now?

A: My abuser was my stepfather, and he died while I was a teenager.

Q: How has this impacted your children and your ability to allow them to spend time with other adults, especially when they were younger?

A: Being abused has significantly affected me as I parent my children, particularly when they were younger. My children rarely have been allowed to spend time at anyone's house during the day, and they never spend

*Name changed for privacy.

91

the night anywhere. I can count on both hands the number of times they have even spent at their grand-parents' house and that was based on a major need for a sitter. That need was my honeymoon and the death of my husband's father. I have allowed my daughter to spend the night at her aunt's house because her aunt is a single parent with a daughter the same age.

I did not explain to my children why they couldn't visit others until they were much older. But I attempt-ed to balance their activities with children their age by allowing them to have company at my home whenever they desired. I realized that I treated my daughter and son differently. My daughter could not have company unless I was at home. This was to protect my husband and son from any allegations from anyone's child vis-iting. However, I felt comfortable with my son having company, even in the presence of my daughter. My family placed major emphasis on depending and lean-ing on each other. My son is older and fiercely protec-tive of his sister, and I felt comfortable that nothing could happen to her in his presence.

Q: Many victims believe that because intercourse did not take place they were not molested. Please share your thoughts on this.

A: My sister, who is a year younger than I, was en-tering into kindergarten in September 1977. While my mother went to meet the teacher, I was introduced to how to effectively have oral sex. Even as a kid, I knew this was not right, and my being forced into learning how to please a man at my age was not at the top of my to-do list. I was touched, probed, and forced for seven years to make my stepfather feel good. I had semen shot in my mouth more times than I can number. My step-father used to tell me all the time that I gave the best "blow job" and that someday I would make a man very happy. He told me that having oral sex with men would never get me pregnant. Although I didn't tell anyone, I always knew this behavior was not acceptable.

Q: Why didn't you tell?

A: My stepfather promised me that he would kill my mother if I said a word. He also said that I would be the one taken away from the home, not him. My stepfather was very abusive physically and suffered mentally after returning from the Vietnam War. I truly believed that he would keep his promise. Also, I knew my oldest sister was suffering just as much as I was, so I felt that if we were sacrifices, the baby of the family would be spared. Years later I found out that everyone, except for his biological daughter, was subject to his cruelty.

Q: How was it revealed, and how has this affected your family as a whole?

A: I was not the one to expose our family secret. My oldest sister finally ran away from home and went to live with our biological father. One day she had a dispute with my mother and out of anger told our dark family secret. The interesting thing was that by that time my mother had already left my stepfather and was moving on with her life. Before all of this, shortly after I graduated from the eighth grade, she and my stepfather had

had an altercation that made her pack up our belong-ings in one hour, and we moved into our grandfather's house. It was during this time that my mother asked me if I had been abused, and finally I said, "yes."

I thought that at that time, my family would begin to heal, but it was my mother who made me feel like what happened to me was my fault. With questions like, "Why didn't you say anything?" "What do you want me to do now?" Statements like, "You'll get over it," and "Let's move on," were more hurting and permanently damaging. I thought the sacrifice of my body for her life would have been more appreciated because I really thought my stepfather would have killed my mother. After all, we lived in a house that was full of violence, drugs, and alcohol abuse.

To know me is to know that I have a very strong per-sonality. While I recognize many people who suffer from abuse blame themselves, I have never accepted that it was my fault. I never questioned what I did to deserve this fate; I always channeled my anger at my stepfather and him alone. While my sisters and I have bonded and grown, my relationship with my mother continues to remain tepid. I have always wanted my mother to ac-knowledge her hand in our abuse. If only she had been home more; if she had stopped the physical abuse, then maybe she would not have left us alone with him so much. If only she had stood up to my stepfather, maybe we would have been a real family. If only she cared.

I realize that I am the only sister out of the three of us that refuses to sweep it under the rug and consider it over. I want my mother to acknowledge and express some remorse over what happened to me. It was not my fault, and I refuse to believe that it was my responsibility to stop the abuse. With my desire to demand an apology, our relationship has weakened significantly. I'm not certain what I can do to strengthen our relationship, but I have forgiven both my stepfather and my mother. However, I refuse to submit myself to be blamed for childhood experiences that I had no control over. Yes, I could have done something. I could have run away. As a matter of fact, I tried that and was sent back home. I could have told my mother, my pastor, my teacher, or social services, but I didn't.

Q: How did it affect you growing up, and what effects have it had on you as an adult?

A: I tried being a straight "A" student in school, but somehow I still managed to always stay on punishment. I felt that my stepfather was keeping me on punishment just so that I would be available to satisfy his needs. The punishments brought a lot of negative attention my way. I always felt that if I remained in the spotlight, people would see that I was being abused. I didn't know how, but I was hoping someone would see the pain, the hurt, the anger, the need for attention, and they would stop and investigate what was going on with me. Still today, with everything that I do, I find myself vying and struggling with the desire to be the center of attention. For years I was the center of unwanted attention, and now I want to know what merited attention feels like.

Back then, and still today, my relief has been found in going to church. My stepfather never stopped me from going to church, so I went whenever the doors were open. It helped me grow tremendously, and I now channel my energy into helping others. I share my experience with others who have been abused physically, mentally, and emotionally in order to help them overcome adversity. If my life can serve as a beacon of light, then my experiences during my childhood would not have been in vain. I believe that my life is truly a testimony, and in spite of every test and trial of my past, I am at peace. I'm married to a husband that understands my pain, and I no longer suffer from the residual effects of being abused. I am loved and nurtured by people whom I feel appreciate me for who I am and not what I can do for them.

One final note, since I began going to church, I truly learned about the Lord being a Comforter and One who answers prayer. I prayed for a spouse who would understand me intimately and not consider me damaged goods. I prayed for a spouse who would love me unconditionally and would support me as I desired to conquer the world. The Lord answered my prayers, and I've never felt inhibited in my sex life. Almost 20 years later, and the sex just continues to get better. Truly I am blessed.

"It seems like I was in and out of the hospital all the time. I remember having my first Pap smear during one of those appointments. The results showed that I was infected with gonorrhea. I was only nine years old."

Elizabeth's* Story

Q: How old were you when it began and how long did it last?

A: I was six when it began and nine when it ended.

Q: Was sexual intercourse or oral sex ever involved?

A: Sexual intercourse as well as oral sex was involved in almost every occasion. I remember looking back at that time in my life and knowing that I didn't have a clue what was going on, but I knew something wasn't right. Even today it sends chills through my body to reflect back and think about those grown men having strong, sexual intercourse with a child. I was molested by my father's stepbrother and nephew over a long period of time. My uncle was around 30 and my cousin was 21.

I would hate going to my grandmother's during the summer because it was nothing more than a house of perverted men who were engaging in strong sex acts with children under the age of 14. The sad thing is that my grandparents' house was an old farmhouse with floors that squeaked with every little move. It always amazed me that Grandma could tell us to stop running around upstairs during the day because of the noise

*Name changed for privacy.

the floors made, but she could never hear how her son and grandson would take each of us into their rooms every night and rotate having sex with all four of us.

I still remember the smell of sex and of lying in semen night after night. My cousin would call me up to his room in the day, and there he stood naked and masturbating. He would make me get on my knees, and he would place his penis in my mouth. He would hold my head and tell me to swallow. He would then perform oral sex on me and then have sex with me. It was so painful because he inserted his full penis into me. I was just a little girl, and he would grind me like I was a grown woman. Sweat would pour from his face, and he would tell me how good my vagina felt to him. He would say to me, "Your vagina is good. One day some man will enjoy your vagina." However, "vagina" definitely wasn't the word he used.

Q: How was it revealed?

A: I began to experience complications when I urinated. I went to the doctor, and that began a series of medical appointments. After that first visit, it seems like I was in and out of the hospital all the time. I remember having my first Pap smear during one of those appointments. The results showed that I was infected with gonorrhea. I was only nine years old.

Q: What effect did this have on you as a teenager and young adult?

A: I didn't date very much. I was afraid of getting into serious relationships because I felt like I would get hurt. The one boy that I did hook up with was only after me for sex and not a relationship. I gave it to him whenever and wherever he wanted it, including parked cars and abandoned houses. I was 14 and he was 19 and already in a relationship with another girl. Our relationship ended very quickly because I realized that he didn't want me for anything but sex, and he wasn't leaving his girlfriend. I didn't date too much after that because I felt awkward; I didn't know how to approach anyone. I was very popular and active in school, but when it came down to relationships I shied away from anything serious.

Q: Why didn't you tell?

A: I can remember not telling anyone because I just knew I did something bad, and I felt that it was my fault. After my physician and parents learned of my having gonorrhea, my mother took me into a private room at the doctor's office and asked me who did this to me. I asked her if she was going to spank me if I told. My mother said, "No, you are not going to get a spanking for telling the truth." I told her it was my uncle and cousin, and I remember how her countenance dropped; it all made sense to her. He was always volunteering to babysit us children.

Q: Did you ever blame yourself or think that maybe you provoked it?

A: I did blame myself. For years, and even still today, I'm learning how to love the person I see in the mirror. The way I used to deal with the abuse was to imagine myself being another person. I never liked the person in the mirror because that person was molested. I thought that if I looked like someone else that person could be happy because they weren't abused. It took over 20 years for me to love the beautiful girl in the mirror and to realize that it wasn't her fault.

Q: Have you forgiven your abusers, and what is your relationship with them like now?

A: I have forgiven the abusers, but I don't trust them even to this day. I have young children and I told them about the abuse. There may be occasions, such as funerals or reunions, where they see these individuals, and I've instructed them to not hug anyone or sit in anyone's lap. They know to always go to bathroom in groups. Other than these family occasions, my family doesn't have a relationship with my offenders.

Q: Did you ever receive counseling?

A: I was 24 when I had my first counseling session. My supervisor at that time read a paper that I had written in college for a project concerning my years of sexual abuse. We began to discuss the fact that I never received any counseling for the abuse, and she suggested that I utilize the free services that our employer offered. I was so scared and reluctant at first because I didn't want to tell anyone my business. I was also concerned about what my church family would think about my going to see a *shrink*. At the time, I didn't have my faith and trust in the Lord. But for the first time in my life I wanted to do something to make me feel better. I began my sessions, and I was able to open up about the past. The best thing that happened in the sessions was I was able to speak to that little girl and tell her that all those things that happened to her were not her fault. You can forgive yourself, love yourself, and LIVE!

Chapter Ten

FAQ
(Frequently Asked Questions)

"Any and all discussions about anything of a sexual nature seem to be taboo, but we must talk about things in a way to keep our children from becoming a victim or a perpetrator."

Q: What do you see as the most common side effect of sexual abuse?

A: There are so many, and they manifest differently in each victim. However, some common effects are:

- Shame, guilt, and poor self-esteem (self concept)

- Sexuality Issues—promiscuity, gender identity issues, or absence of appropriate intimate relationships

- In children: acting out sexually with other children

Q: Are the side effects for males and females usually the same?

A: No, males are much more likely to act out (externalize) with disruptive behaviors, fighting, rape, or even self-abusive behaviors. Girls are more likely to act in (internalize) and become depressed or anxious. Boys are under pressure to be tough or macho.

Q: How do most victims respond to counseling and treatment?

A: Well, I have difficulty with "most" victims as all victims bring so many differences to treatment. First, it is imperative to note that counseling and treatment range along a continuum from most restrictive to least restrictive. Most restrictive would be in-patient hospitalization. This form of treatment is necessary when a victim is a danger to self, others, or property. Least restrictive would be out-patient counseling once weekly or a support group. What I have found over the years for children in counseling is that they will respond well through the use of play therapy, coloring, and games. They will disclose information only when they feel safe. Amazingly, safety is important with adults as well. However, adults generally come for help when they are in crisis. After they feel better they will stop coming for counseling even if the treatment is not done. So, I explain at the beginning how therapy will go, and if they want long-term resolve, completion of the sessions is imperative.

Q: Do you feel counseling is necessary for all sexual abuse victims?

A: I feel it can only be helpful, and there are several reasons why:

1. Counseling can create a safe place to talk openly about ALL feelings, thoughts, behaviors, etc.

2. Counseling can provide an opportunity to educate the victim about the thoughts, feelings, and behaviors associated with sexual abuse.

3. Counseling can help the victim discover and control triggers. Triggers are sounds, smells, tastes, feelings, and visuals that take the victim back to the incident or remind them of the place, person, etc.... I had a client who was an extremely talented pianist but never played. She was sexually abused by her piano instructor, and sitting at the piano is a trigger.

4. Counseling can assist the victim in understanding that as he or she matriculates through the normal stages of life development, new issues may surface and a couple of counseling sessions may be necessary.

5. Effective counseling can help remove the stigma that most people have about going for professional help. Counseling does not mean you are "crazy." Within certain cultural groups, this is a prevailing belief. They may perceive seeking help as weak, crazy, etc.... However, mental health is just one part of our overall health, and God's Word says, "Beloved, I wish above all things that thou mayest prosper and be in health, even as thy soul prospereth" (3 John 2). Our total health is physical, mental, and spiritual.

Q: Families are going to connect and spend time together, and there will be instances when adults are not always around to watch over their children. However, child on child sexual abuse is a major problem. I like to refer to it as "kissing cousins."

What can we do to address this issue specifically?

A: This is a problem with a huge impact. Most child sexual abuse happens within families. The first thing all families must do is remove the secrecy. Any and all discussions about anything of a sexual nature seem to be taboo, but we must talk about things in a way to keep our children from becoming a victim or a perpetrator. All children must be educated about appropriate and inappropriate touch. Also, never leave the kids in rooms alone with the doors closed for long periods of time. It only takes a couple of seconds for inappropriate activities to occur. Always check on them! As adults, we have the responsibility to keep our children safe, even from each other.

Q: When a child is molested, they're not the only victim. The whole family is victimized. What steps can a family take together to bring healing to everyone?

A: The whole family must own their feelings and get counseling where everyone is in the session together. If the whole family goes for help, it supports the victim and does not single him or her out as the "one" with the problem. Also, it helps the victim feel protected. The counseling should address anger management, conflict resolution, problem solving skills, empathy training, effective communication, and discussion of any feelings of guilt the adults may have.

Q: There's a myth that only females are sexually abused. That is far from the truth. Share with us some insight about what's happening to our young men. Who are their abusers?

A: Boys are sexually abused, and the numbers are climbing. One out of 3 girls is sexually abused before the age of 16 and 1 out of 5 boys is sexually abused before the age 16. There are many things we need to understand about the abuse of boys:

• Men who are sexually abused as children are twice as likely to become substance abusers, commit suicide, be prone to illness, have problems in school, and be antisocial or overly aggressive, and verbally or physically abusive to their mates.

• Sexual assault of boys by females is grossly under reported due to the perception of boys being made into men when they are sexed by a woman. Women account for 20 percent of the sexual abuse of boys.

• Boys are harmed by having sexual contact with an adult of either gender.

• A little known fact is that the sexual arousal that results from fondling or stroking a pre-pubescent boy's genitals rapidly produces extreme pain since he is incapable at that age of reaching an orgasm. This is sexual torture.

• Sexual assaults on boys tend to be more violent and are more likely to result in serious physical injury or death than those perpetrated on females.

Q: Besides the fact that sexual abusers are usually people who were sexually abused themselves, what are some other reasons that men and women become sexual abusers?
A: The reasons behind why a person becomes an

active sexual abuser can be a combination of many things, but all require intervention and help.

1. There are people who are pedophiles, and they are just attracted to children. This is a mental illness and is listed in the *Diagnostic and Statistical Manual of Mental Disorders (DSM IV)*. This is a very difficult pill to swallow, but it is necessary to look at how you are attracted to what you are attracted to. You will not change that without some traumatic occurrence. The same thing is true for the pedophiles. They do not see what they do as harming a child. Because they love the child, they romance the child, etc....

2. While some offenders seek sexual gratification from the act, most times it is more about power, control, and anger.

3. The non-predatory molester tends to be men whose primary sexual attraction is towards adults, but he may molest children in a maladaptive attempt to meet emotional needs.

Evangelist Sabrina Jackson, MSW, is a clinical therapist with over 15 years experience working with children, adults, and families. Ms. Jackson is a highly sought-after speaker who speaks internationally on various topics, all of which bring healing to the mind, body, and spirit.

Contact: 1-800-498-9210 or www.sabrinajackson. com.

PART IV

HEALING AND WHOLENESS

Chapter Eleven

Goodbye

How Do You Leave Here?

Across the board, it is common for people who have been sexually abused and those who treat them to use the word "survivor" instead of "victim." I think this is great. Someone who has experienced sexual abuse is indeed a survivor. However, I use the word "victim" often. I believe that if a person has never faced what happened to them and they're still allowing for it to dominate their life, they're still being "*victimized*" by the past. This is why getting on the right path to healing and wholeness is so important.

We began this journey with the question: "How did I get here?" I know that my story is the story of millions of people. Sure, there may be some differences in how things took place, but for the most part, many of us have found ourselves in the same situation—abused, hurt, and desperate for answers and for freedom from the bondage of the past. We have now made it to the most important part of all: "How do *you* leave here?"

• BUILD A RELATIONSHIP WITH GOD

God saved me! When I began to cry out to God and He heard my voice, the healing process began. I received understanding of what the Bible means when it says, "With His (Jesus) stripes, we are healed" (Isaiah 53:5). I remember a time when my pastor preached for several months on healing. Although I was dealing with some physical issues, my soul also was being healed. I would buy copies of the sermons, and I would listen to them over and over again. I developed a strong prayer life, and I would talk to God about how brokenhearted I was, how scared I was about my husband abandoning me, and how ashamed I was about my past. Slowly, but surely, the healing process began to take place. I began to meditate on scriptures about God's love for me and about healing and forgiveness. I went after the Word of God at all cost. I staked my life on it.

Change didn't come overnight. As a matter of fact, there are still things that I battle with today. I didn't get a *sudden* revelation of who God is and then all of a sudden my life changed. It has been an ongoing healing process for me. I am a work in progress. However, things have changed! I stand firm on the promises of God that my victory is here. No, it hasn't been an easy process, and there were some really rough days in the beginning where I was balled up in bed with snot tissue all over my face and sheets. I would cry and pray. That's all I could do at the time, just cry and pray. Eventually, though, the crying stopped, and my prayers grew stronger. I'm not saying that everyone has to go through this same process, but this is what it took for me. Going through the healing process may be extremely difficult for some people and not for others, but one thing is for sure; you can't do it without God!

• SURROUND YOURSELF WITH POSITIVE PEOPLE

I can't leave out the support of my family. My husband kept me encouraged from the beginning, and he continues to support the work that I do today. He's always told me go out and talk about it so that I could help someone else dealing with this issue. He didn't shun me or make me feel bad. He let me cry when I needed to cry, but he also kept telling me to get up and do something about it. That's exactly what I did. I let go of the pride, disowned the shame, and I began to go out and share my story of tragedy to triumph with others. I removed the veil that I had hidden behind for so many years. I've allowed God to turn my mess into a ministry. Because of this, each day gets better, lives are being changed, and families are being healed.

• LET YOUR SOUL BE HEALED

Although abuse takes place as a physical act on the outside, the emotional and mental scars run deep. While there are few cases of physical evidence of sexual abuse, the effects are mostly internal and are acted out externally. Therefore, a complete emotional and mental healing must take place. Your soul must be healed. Victims tend to think that because it happened when they were young, it will just go away. That's rarely the case. In some way, shape, or form, it will affect a victim's life. That's why you must stop its effects before they stop you from being the great man or woman that you're destined to be.

• PRAYER

I believe in the power of prayer! It's not some hit or miss act in my life. When I pray, I expect results. Therefore, I'm always praying for my family, including those who offended me. I pray for their health, love, peace, joy, salvation, prosperity and complete healing of their own souls. I want them to get better because I do realize that there's something wrong in their lives. Many sexual offenders are people who were victimized in their own childhood and never received help. I pray that they'll get help and get better.

Some people might think that they don't know how to pray, but prayer is simply a conversation with God. We can talk to Him just like we talk to our families and friends. Some days all I could conjure up was enough strength to just call His name. There were times that all I could say was "Jesus!" It worked!

• TELL SOMEONE

I think talking to someone is one of the most important steps that a victim can take. Talk to a good friend, parent or guardian, teacher, counselor or minister. It helps to lean on others and cry on their shoulders, but you must talk to someone who is going to move you to action and not just give you permission to have a pity

party. This doesn't need to be someone whose only response will be, "Wow! That really happened to you?"

When we don't break the silence in our families, we are allowing it to go on generation after generation. There are people in my family who are several years younger than I who were molested, and some of them by the same individuals that were molesting me. I can see the effects on their lives: drugs, alcoholism, unwanted pregnancies, abortions, poverty, crime, promiscuity, anger, and I could go on. Had I said something, there could have been a different outcome.

Fern Johnson, a friend of mine, said, "When you come forth you may not get the response you initially want." I'm now telling you not to be surprised if you don't always get the sympathy and understanding that you're looking for. Since you are the abuse victim, it would seem that everyone would have compassion and embrace you with open arms, but that won't always happen. Some people are going to be mad at you. "How can you do this to our family?" They'll ask. But I ask: How can you not? How can you not protect the lives of the ones you love?

It's important for you to have compassion because the healing process may be hard on the entire family. There are many issues involved once the silence has finally been broken. Parents might find themselves trying to explain to their children why they suddenly can't visit their favorite aunt or uncle, or why they can't play with Nana or Grandpa anymore. This alone can create a lot of hurt and confusion. People in the family might accuse you of having deceptive motives

or seeking attention. Others may call you a liar. Be prepared for it all! My family has been very supportive, but not everyone had nice things to say to me. While I know that all of this is very difficult for them to deal with, I believe that everyone was tired of keeping the secret. You must believe that in the end the healing that takes place will far outweigh anyone's opinion of you.

I had a small surprise of my own when I spoke to a group of young ladies at a community center. It was the first time I didn't get the response that I had expected and had become accustomed to. Most of them were angry with me, accusing me of lying. They asked how could I not have known what was going on, and they called me stupid for forgiving my abusers. They couldn't seem to understand how I could be around those who offended me and say that I still love them. I had to explain to them about the power of forgiveness and walking in love, especially to one young lady who admitted that she had been abused and confessed that she was just waiting until she got old enough to kill her abuser. During this same session, I also had to embrace another young girl who became so overwhelmed with guilt about the abuse she had experienced, she stormed out of the room yelling and crying.

SEEK PROFESSIONAL HELP

Although I had the opportunity to sit with a few ministers over the years, I never received formal counseling. However, I did receive what I consider the best counseling in the world. When I began to face what happened to me I was employed in a position that

allowed me to wear headphones. Instead of listening to music CDs or the radio, I would listen to sermons. I bought every message my pastor and other ministers at my church preached. I listened to them for 8 to 10 hours each day. It was the only thing that played in my car and in my home. For at least half of each day I heard, *"Stephanie, you're healed. Stephanie, you are an overcomer. Stephanie, you have all power through Christ Jesus. Stephanie, you are victorious. Stephanie, no weapon formed against you shall prosper."* If you hear someone telling you that you are uniquely and wonderfully made, prosperous, loved, and powerful over and over again every day of your life, eventually you'll begin to believe it, and you'll begin to act like it. The abuse and the negative thoughts that I had about myself, which were implanted in my spirit over a long period of time, had to be replaced with good thoughts.

However, your situation or your child's situation may be different. Some people need formal counseling to help them sort through their pain. A counselor can help pull out all of the garbage that's hidden deep within. Counselors ask the tough questions that a person may not consider on his or her own. That's one of the great benefits that I have with helping other people deal with sexual abuse. They sometimes ask me really tough questions that even I have to think and pray about. It helps prepare me for situations that a victim may have dealt with that I didn't. Another great benefit to counseling is that you have someone right there to comfort you or say the right words at the right time. Seeking professional help doesn't mean that a person is crazy.

In fact, it's just the opposite; they are trying to avoid reaching that point of insanity. I personally think that going to counseling is a brave move. It's a person saying: *"Look, I'm dealing with something, and I want help so that I can be a better person."* That takes courage!

• Do Not Live In Fear

Many sexual abuse victims live their lives in fear. They're afraid to get married. They're afraid to trust a man or a woman. They're afraid to be alone. Some people have so much fear in their hearts that they fail to allow their children breathing room. If you have been sexually abused and you now have children, don't rob them of their childhood because of what happened to you. You must allow them to enjoy life and interact with other people, especially with other children. You just have to do it with wisdom and caution. God has not given anyone the spirit of fear. Fear is a learned behavior, and you don't have to accept it.

• Stop Blaming Yourself and Let Go of the Guilt

I can't stress enough that abuse is not the victim's fault. Whether a child was 6 years old or 12 when it began, it was not his or her fault. The child was the victim of a crime, and must release the guilt.

• Forgive Yourself

When I talk about forgiving yourself, I'm not talking about for the abuse. You were a victim and have nothing to forgive as far as that is concerned. However, if there is any shred of guilt for not telling someone about it, you must let it go. I spent some time beating myself up for not telling, but that time is over, and it has passed away forever. I had to move on and let go of any guilt I felt for not protecting other children in the family. Forgiving ourselves is a hard thing to do, yet we are able to forgive everyone around us for all of their mistakes. We talk to them about moving on but when it comes to ourselves, we don't have that same mercy and compassion. We beat ourselves down because we don't feel worthy of forgiveness. Well, God is no respecter of persons. You are due the same grace and mercy that I am. Grab hold of it!

• FORGIVE THOSE WHO OFFENDED YOU

"Forgiveness is a decision, not a feeling."
—Pastor Duane Vander Klok

Wow was the only reaction I could come up with when I heard Pastor Duane Vander Klok say, "Forgiveness is a decision, not a feeling." Hearing this really helped me understand my ability to forgive those who had sexually abused me, especially with so many people thinking that I am crazy for doing so. Unforgiveness eats away at the soul. It leaves a person trapped in the past and unable to move forward. Unforgiveness will never change anything. I've made the decision to forgive. Besides, I wanted to forgive them. I was tired of being angry at people.

Even if you commit to hating a person until the day you take your last breath, the fact that the abuse happened will not change. Your offenders will go on with their lives, most often pretending like it never happened, and you'll sit back seething and stressing yourself out. This level of stress creates sickness and disease in the body. Hate and unforgiveness has never made anything better, and it never will. One important thing to understand is that forgiving someone doesn't mean that you must have a relationship with that person. It simply means that you're able to let it go and move on with your life. I have a relationship and fellowship with some of my offenders, but that is my choice. I'm able to do so without any bitterness in my heart. But everyone's situation is not the same. Regardless of what type of relationship you have with them, you must learn to forgive them in your heart.

• LET GO OF THE PAIN—MOVE ON!

The affliction of my youth has not prevailed against me. Yes, it kept me bound and confused for many years, but not any longer. Today I am a confident and loving woman. Sure, there are still some things that I'm dealing with, but that's okay. I'm not afraid to say that I am a work in progress and I'm constantly working on my life. At one point, I felt that because I had done so many terrible things in the past, I wasn't worthy of forgiveness or happiness. I felt as if I couldn't move on. But over time I learned to let go of the pain and get on with my life. I really am a new person. Only for the purpose of helping someone else do I ever think about the abuse at all. My youth has been renewed.

• FORGET A PLAN B!

It's amazing how God sometimes speaks to us. I received a promotional flyer in the mail from a bank that asked the question, "Do you have a Plan B?" Although the flyer was referring to investment strategies and retirement planning, it got me to thinking about myself. I said to myself, "Well, there's no Plan B for me."

There's no Plan B for you either. You are God's Plan A. I don't care how much makeup you put on. You can have things on your body stuffed, shaped, cut, botoxed, plucked and tucked, and it won't change who you are. There is no amount of money in the world that can buy another you. I don't care how far the world advances in technology or how many scientific discoveries are made, there is absolutely nothing in this world that can replace you. You can't be cloned. There will never be another person in this world who walks, talks, laughs, cries, thinks, eats, sleeps, and breathes exactly the way you do. There's something powerful in realizing and accepting this. You are special! There's no Plan B for your life.

• KNOW YOUR VALUE

Surround yourself with positive people, only those who bring joy into your life. Get rid of the dream killers. It's like nationally renowned motivational speaker George Fraser says, "Introduce me to your five closest friends, and that will tell me who you are." You don't need to be around anyone who is going to look down on you or talk down to you. You don't need to be around anyone who is going to judge and ridicule your family. You don't need to be around people who are just interested in getting all up in your family's business, trying to find out who did what. This doesn't mean that you have to stop talking to people, but you may have to distance yourself from certain people. God is love. You are made in God's image, so you are love. You need love!

PART V

RESOURCES

Finding Help

Childhelp®

Founded in 1959 by Sara O'Meara and Yvonne Fedderson, Childhelp® is a leading national non-profit organization dedicated to helping victims of child abuse and neglect. Childhelp's® approach focuses on prevention, intervention and treatment. The Childhelp® National Child Abuse Hotline, 1-800-4-A-CHILD, operates 24 hours a day, seven days a week, and receives calls from throughout the United States, Canada, the U.S. Virgin Islands, Puerto Rico and Guam.

http://www.childhelpusa.org

Child Welfare Information Gateway
Protecting Children Strengthening Families

Formerly the National Clearinghouse on Child Abuse and Neglect Information and the National Adoption Information Clearinghouse, Child Welfare Information Gateway provides access to information and resources to help protect children and strengthen families. It is a service of the Children's Bureau, Administration for Children and Families, U.S. Department of Health and Human Services.

1-800-394-3366 or http://www.childwelfare.gov/contact.cfm

124 • T_{HE} E_{NEMY} B_{ETWEEN} M_Y L_{EGS}

National Center for Missing & Exploited Children® (NCMEC)

The National Center for Missing & Exploited Children's® mission is to help prevent child abduction and sexual exploitation, help find missing children, and assist victims of child abduction and sexual exploitation, their families, and the professionals who serve them. 24-Hour Hotline: 1-800-THE-LOST (1-800-843-5678) or http://www.missingkids.com

RAINN (Rape, Abuse & Incest National Network)

The Rape, Abuse & Incest National Network is the nation's largest anti-sexual assault organization and has been ranked as one of "America's 100 Best Charities" by *Worth* magazine. Among its programs, RAINN created and operates the National Sexual Assault Hotline at 1-800-656-HOPE. This nationwide partnership of more than 1,100 local rape treatment hotlines provides victims of sexual assault with free, confidential services around the clock. The hotline helped 137,039 sexual assault victims in 2005 and has helped more than one million since it began in 1994.

Sabrina Jackson Enterprises
Sabrina Jackson, MSW

1-800-498-9210 or www.sabrinajackson.com

Stop the Silence®

Stop the Silence® is a non-profit, charitable 501(c) 3 organization working with others toward the prevention and treatment of child sexual abuse.

http://www.stopcsa.org

Books to Read

Battlefield of the Mind
By Joyce Meyer

Beauty to Ashes
By Joyce Meyer

Hush
By Nicole Braddock Bromley

No Secrets, No Lies: How Black Families Can Heal from Sexual Abuse
By Robin D. Stone

Woman Thou Art Loosed
By Bishop TD Jakes

Help For Sexual Abuse Offenders

What can the offender do to get help? Sexual abuse offenders not only need help, but they also need to deal with the root cause of their problems. This is a subject matter that needs addressing on its own. However, I believe that there is someone reading this book right now who has found him or herself on the other side of the fence as the one who is or who has actually committed the offense of sexual abuse. I would like to offer a few steps for the offender to take that can begin the healing process in his or her own life.

- Do not be afraid to seek help. Counseling or therapy is available to you. If you can't afford to go to a professional therapist or psychologist, or if you prefer to do so, visit your local church. Talk to a minister. Whatever you do, get help now!

- Forgive yourself. We all have done things that we are not proud of. I know that I have. Regardless of who you are or what you've done, God will forgive you for it, and you should forgive yourself.

- Find the root cause of your problem. This may require you to look into your own past or admit that you have some issues that you have never wanted to deal with before. However, you must pluck the weed up by the root. If not, it will keep growing back and manifest in other areas of your life or cause you to continue to abuse and hurt the ones you love.

The Enemy Between My Legs
Readers's Survey
(Three Basic Questions)

1. Have you ever been sexually abused?

☐ Yes   ☐ No

2. If yes, who was your abuser?

☐ Mother   ☐ Father   ☐ Sister

☐ Brother   ☐ Aunt   ☐ Uncle

☐ Babysitter   ☐ Teacher

☐ Friend of the family

☐ Other_____

3. Did you tell someone?

☐ Yes   ☐ No

Please feel free to share your story and any additional information. *All information will be kept confidential.*

_____

_____

_____

_____

_____

_____

_____

_____

_____

_____

_____

_____

_____

_____

_____

_____

_____

_____

OPTIONAL:

Name: _____

Mailing Address: _____

Email Address: _____

**Mail to: Stephanie L. Jones, P.O. Box 401363,
Redford, MI 48240**

You may also contact me online at
www.stephanieljones.com.

Notes

Chapter Four: Who, What, When, Where, And Why?

1. Stop It Now!, "Is child sexual abuse really that big of a problem?", http://www.stopitnow.com/comquest.html

2. Breakthrough Options, "My child would tell me.", http://www.breakthroughoptions.com/id14.html

3. Crimes Against Children Research Center, "Don't count anyone out!", http://www.unh.edu/ccrc/factsheet/pdf/CSA-FS20.pdf

4. Childabuse.com, "Sex Offenders: Who Are They?", http://www.childabuse.com/fs19.htm

5. Stop It Now!, "Kissing Cousins: Do children abuse other children?", http://www.stopitnow.com/csa-facts.html

6. Childabuse.com, "Are your parents really your heroes?", http://www.childabuse.com/fs19.htm

Chapter Five: Knowing Is Half The Battle

7. Braveheart.org, Exposure and Common Signs, http://www.braveheart.org/risk.php

8. Stop It Now!, "Common signs of sexual abuse," http://www.stopitnow.com/warnings.html

9. Stop It Now!, "What to watch for in an adult or older child." http://www.stopitnow.com/warnings.html#watchout

Chapter Six: Protecting The Ones You Love

10. U.S. Department of Justice Office of Justice Programs, Crimes Against Children by Babysitters, "Sexual abuse and daycare centers," http://www. ncjrs.gov/pdffiles1/ojjdp/189102.pdf

11. Childabuse.com, "Be careful what you let your children watch and listen to.", http://www.childabuse. com/fs19.htm

Chapter Eight: Families Under Siege—Consequences Of Sexual Abuse

12. Family Research Council, "Homosexuality and Lesbianism, http://www.frc.org/get.cfm?i=WA03I35

13. Childhelp, "Gateway to Other Destructive Behaviors, htp://www.childhelp.org/resources/learning-center/statistics

14. National Clearinghouse on Child Abuse and Neglect Information: Long-term Consequences of Child Abuse & Neglect, 2005

15. Associated Content, "Teen Pregnancy," http:// www.associatedcontent.com/article/271612/the_ teen_pregnancy_epidemic_the_light_.html

16. EzineArticles.com, Dorothy M. Neddermeyer, PhD, "Teen Pregnancy," http://www.ezinearticles.com/ ?expert=Dorothy_M._Neddermeyer.phd

About the Author

Stephanie ~ Meaning: The Crowned One

*Bless the Lord, O my soul: and all that is
within me, bless his holy name. Bless the
Lord, O my soul, and forget not all his benefits:
Who forgiveth all thine iniquities; who healeth
all thy diseases; Who redeemeth thy life
from destruction; who "crowneth" thee with
lovingkindness and tender mercies; Who
satisfieth thy mouth with good things; so that
"thy youth is renewed like the eagle's."*
—Psalm 103:1-5, quotations mine

Stephanie L. Jones opted out of corporate America
after spending several years working for Fortune 500
companies. A pursuit of her entrepreneurial goals then
led to a brief career in marketing and public relations.
As a publicist, she worked with and helped to advance
the careers of several bestselling book authors. Although highly successful in her endeavors, she soon
took another bold step, this time to fulfill her destiny.
She became an advocate for individuals suffering from
the effects of child sexual abuse.

Stephanie is known for her honest approach in dealing with sexual abuse, a subject that few people will openly discuss. She has the ability to understand and connect with abuse victims, especially the teenagers and young adults. This has made her a highly sought-after speaker for schools, churches, and major organizations.

Among several other honors, she has received the Kiwanis International Lee Harden Take Time to Care Award for her community service work. She's a volunteer student mentor and works with several organizations whose focus is youth and community development. Stephanie, and her husband, Robert, live in the metro Detroit area.